This one-of-a-kind visual glossary demystifies the complicated, often highfalutin language of wine. Lessons include:

- *Tasting terms to describe first impressions, aroma, flavor, acidity, texture and mouthfeel, condition, and personality—with example sentences that will make you wine smart*

- *Necessary information for basic topics of conversation, like the difference between filtered and unfiltered wines and when to refer to a wine as Old World or New World*

- *Introductory guides on topics like glassware, sparkling wines, fermentation vessels, and more*

- *A wine pairing cheat sheet*

- *Drinking games to put your knowledge to the test*

- *And much more!*

No other book provides such an entertaining deep dive into wine lingo. Learn what to say and how to say it, and sound effortlessly wine smart every sip of the way.

HOW TO SOUND
WINE
SMART

HOW TO SOUND

WINE SMART

AN ILLUSTRATED GUIDE

WRITTEN AND ILLUSTRATED BY

MARYSE CHEVRIERE

SIMON ELEMENT

NEW YORK   AMSTERDAM/ANTWERP   LONDON   TORONTO
SYDNEY/MELBOURNE   NEW DELHI

SIMON
ELEMENT

An Imprint of Simon & Schuster, LLC
1230 Avenue of the Americas
New York, NY 10020

First Simon Element hardcover edition July 2026

SIMON ELEMENT is a registered trademark of Simon & Schuster, LLC

For information about special discounts for bulk purchases, please contact Simon & Schuster Special Sales at 1-866-506-1949 or business@simonandschuster.com.

The Simon & Schuster Speakers Bureau can bring authors to your live event. For more information or to book an event, contact the Simon & Schuster Speakers Bureau at 1-866-248-3049 or visit our website at www.simonspeakers.com.

Interior design by Jen Wang

Manufactured in China

10 9 8 7 6 5 4 3 2 1

Library of Congress Control Number: 2025939505

ISBN 978-1-6680-8776-3
ISBN 978-1-6680-8777-0 (ebook)

Let's stay in touch! Scan here to get book recommendations, exclusive offers, and more delivered to your inbox.

For Mom, who's always made me believe that I could achieve anything. And for Dad, who loved to laugh and inspired me to think outside the box.

Introduction

Raise your hand if you've ever felt personally victimized by a wine nerd.

You know what I'm talking about. You're out to dinner, looking to order a glass, or picking something up at the bottle shop, and the wine nerd chirps, "A dry white? This Chablis is super *lean*, with *screaming* acidity and a powerful *mineral core—like a lemon orchard and a quarry had a love child!*"

Or "This Nebbiolo is in such *a great spot right now*, positively *singing*, with aromatics *jumping out of the glass*. Great *structure*, *grippy* tannins, with *bright, juicy* fruit to balance it out."

You say, "Oh, wow, amazing, sounds great!" But inside you're thinking "*Whaaaat* did I just sign up to drink?"

As one of the offenders, I promise you we're not trying to alienate you (or complicate things or exclude you) when we slip into our sommspeak Parseltongue. But I understand how it can have that effect. I'll be honest: When I dumb-lucked my way into my first wine gig, I had only a shoestring's worth of wine knowledge and certainly was *not* fluent in the lingo.

The words used to capture and communicate what's going on in the glass is a language unto itself. It's complicated, often ridiculous sounding, ever evolving, charged with emotion, and highly subjective. If you're not familiar with it, trying to get at its meaning and really talk about wine—what you're smelling and tasting, how it feels in your mouth, what you like and don't like—can be super intimidating. Or worse: It can make you feel stupid. And that really, truly bums me out. Because at the core, drinking and sharing and talking wine are supposed to be *fun*.

I was incredibly lucky that the place where I got my start in the industry was devoted to making wine less intimidating and more accessible. In a landscape that can all too often feel exclusionary and pretentious and breed impostor syndrome, I think it's an important perspective to continue to promote—*especially* if you want to get new people into wine.

That probably explains why, back in 2015 while tipsily

studying for my Certified Sommelier exam, I thought it would be funny to take a wine-tasting note, turn it into a cartoon, and then share it on Instagram. That note was "Never thought I'd see so many roses in one room." I wasn't familiar with the Piedmontese red it was referring to, but with those few words I felt I got it. I could *see* it. In that moment, it dawned on me just how visually evocative winespeak is and that maybe something as approachable as my simple little doodle could help people become more comfortable with it—or, at the very least, give them a laugh. I wanted to show that wine doesn't have to be so hoity-toity and that wine nerds can indeed have a sense of humor. So that was how @Freshcutgardenhose was born.

Initially when I hunted for tasting notes to draw, I'd always go for the wildest, most roll-your-eyes "Who *talks* like that?" kind of thing. Like "Riding in a giant seashell along a hot sandy beach next to water of stone fruit and tropical music." But as I

continued on in my professional journey, which has included everything from running restaurant wine programs to working in retail shops and tasting rooms, I noticed that what I had become accustomed to as everyday winespeak worked as @Freshcutgardenhose fodder, too. And not just for laughs. Maybe those cartoons could actually help make winespeak easier to understand. And that was where this book, *How to Sound Wine Smart*, came from.

My goal for this book is simple: to give you a one-of-a-kind visual glossary that makes learning how to "speak wine" as entertaining as drinking wine is.

This is not a Wine 101 book. There are already countless great ones out there, and I encourage you to read them as your quest for wine knowledge inspires you to do so. But I've noticed that because the 101s have so much else to cover, they don't usually have the space to deep dive into the lexicon of wine lingo. We'll cover everything from what to say when you take your first big whiff to when you recognize that something might not quite be right and everything in between.

Before we dive in, a quick note on how this book is organized. We'll start off with some must-know basics—most important, how to taste wine and why each step of the process matters. Then we'll get into the vocabulary lessons. (I use the term "lessons" loosely, because the last thing I want is for this to feel like a textbook.) I've divided the lingo into chapters, more or less following the order of how you'd use them when tasting:

- *First impressions and conversation starters*
- *Aroma*
- *Flavor*
- *Acidity*
- *Texture and mouthfeel*
- *Condition*
- *Personality*
- *Faults and flaws*

For each term, an example sentence is provided for inspiration. Sprinkled throughout, you'll also find "Keep Pouring" sections for deeper dives into topics related to the lingo, as well as drinking games to put your knowledge to practical (read: good!) use.

So there you have it. I hope you find this book useful and learn a thing or two, and I hope you have a good time doing it. I hope you will want to come back and reference it time and again when you're enjoying a bottle and working through what you're tasting and how to describe it. We're going to cover a lot of ground here and maybe you won't remember everything, and that's okay. This is one example I can think of where practicing is fun! I hope it makes you feel, as I did when I first started, that wine can indeed be less intimidating, more accessible, and more enjoyable.

Remember, too, that so much of winespeak is subjective. There is no one "right way" to do it. Use this book to help you start to find *your* style. Take from it what speaks to you.

More than anything, I hope this book makes you want to pick up a glass and smile.

Pre–Gaming

Before We Get to Tasting Notes, Some Notes on Tasting

Before we get to the important business of helping you sound as though you know what you're talking about when you're describing wine, we need to address some basics about *tasting* wine. Most important are the standard techniques for how to do it and why each step matters. We'll also go over some glassware good-to-knows, cover the main flavor categories and where they come from, and talk about what some of that info on a wine label means. Let's get this party started.

HOW TO TASTE A GLASS OF WINE

**STEP 1:
LOOK
AT IT.**

Before getting to the fun bit, the sampling, give the wine in your glass a good visual once-over. Preferably, you should be somewhere well lit, angling the glass away from you over a white surface for maximum visibility of color hue and density. I know, I know, life teaches us that we shouldn't judge based on appearances, but when it comes to wine, how it looks can provide a lot of useful clues.

Color.

This can help answer questions such as:

"What grape(s) is it made from?" Different grapes naturally have different pigmentation and skin thickness, which will have an impact on the color of the wine they produce. Pinot Noir, for example, is a thin-skinned grape with less pigmentation that generally produces a wine that's light red in color. It will never look the same as Malbec, which is thick skinned and highly pigmented and produces wine with a vibrant, dark purplish hue. (See page 15 to get an idea of some general color categories and which varieties tend to fall under them.)

Just so we start on the same page: The juice from any grape variety—red or white—is clear. Red wine is red because the pigmented grape skins are macerated with the juice. White

Pale Straw

*Pinot Grigio,
Vinho Verde,
Muscadet*

Medium
Lemon Yellow

*Sauvignon Blanc,
Grüner Veltliner,
Riesling*

Golden

*Oak-aged
Chardonnay,
Marsanne,
Viognier*

Pale Ruby

*Pinot Noir, Gamay,
Frappato, Nebbiolo
(young)*

Medium
Red-Garnet

*Sangiovese, Merlot,
Tempranillo*

Medium-
Deep Purple

*Syrah, Malbec,
Mourvèdre*

Aged White

*Dark brownish-
yellow at rim*

Aged Red

*More pale, orangey,
reddish-brown at rim*

wines are white because the juice is pressed off of the skins. If the juice from white grapes is macerated with the skins, orange (aka skin-contact) wine is produced. Rosé can be made in a few different ways, but often it's done by letting the juice from red grapes spend just a short time macerating on the skins. Make sense?

"How old is it?" White wines get darker and more golden brown as they age, whereas red wines get lighter and more orangey. Look for this color variation at the rim edge of the wine in your glass—the perimeter of the liquid that, as you're angling the glass, would be coming closest to spilling out.

"How was it made/What's the style like?" A white wine that's been aged in oak, for instance, will likely have a deeper, more golden color than one aged in stainless steel because it has been exposed to gentle oxidation. Speaking about style, a red that's lighter and more translucent is usually an indication that it will be lighter bodied and lower alcohol.

Clarity.

Whether a wine is clear or cloudy can also give an indication of how it was made.

Filtered vs. Unfiltered Wine

Wine is made when yeast and sugar (i.e., unfermented grape juice) is converted into alcohol and carbon dioxide (CO_2). When you hear someone say that a wine is "filtered," it just means that the spent yeast particles left over from fermentation (called "lees") and bacteria have been removed. Usually this is done by passing the wine through, you guessed it, some kind of filter. Why is most wine given the Brita treatment? Aesthetics, for one, but also because there's always the risk that leaving some bacteria in the wine can cause it to go off in some way. So in that sense, filtered wines are considered to be more stable.

Of course, those who stand on the other side of the fence would tell you that this stability comes at a price; that the conventional large-scale techniques for filtering and fining can dull and homogenize a wine.

The gray area is that not all unfiltered wines are cloudy. In many cases, a winemaker will allow the lees to settle at the bottom of the fermentation vessel so that the wine can be siphoned off, a process called "racking." It's kind of like straining a broth, where you get rid of the bones and pieces of aromatics and save the clear liquid.

Ultimately, how unfiltered an unfiltered wine is comes down to the discretion of the winemaker and what fits their philosophical and stylistic goals.

CLEAR

This is when you look at the wine in your glass and don't see any particles floating in it. It's transparent. Expect to see this the majority of the time, as most wines are filtered and fined (no, not like a parking ticket; it's a clarification process that removes molecules that could negatively impact the wine's flavor and aroma).

Although common practice among professionals to say when blind tasting—aka, when you try to guess what a wine is by looking at and tasting it—it's not something you really *need* to call out. It's just worth taking note of.

When you observe the liquid in the glass and it looks like your kitchen after an *Oh, #$*@#! I totally forgot there was something in the oven!!* moment. Hazy.

If you see this, you're definitely drinking an unfiltered wine. And chances are, it's a "natural" or "low-intervention" wine. That's because those who practice this style of winemaking believe that commercial methods of filtering and fining can strip away some of a wine's character and uniqueness. (Not to make things too confusing, but it's important to note that not all natural wines are cloudy, because not all unfiltered wines are cloudy. So if you come across a natural wine that's clear, don't be alarmed; that doesn't mean it's fake news.)

Cloudy wines are a lot less common than clear wines, so pointing it out in a tasting note makes sense. Mostly, think of it as a visual clue as to the style of the wine and winemaking philosophy of the producer.

CLOUDY

STEP 2:
SMELL IT.

Hold your glass up to your nose and give the wine a quick whiff. Then give the wine a swirl and stick your nose back in there, taking a big sniff this time. No, the swirl is not just for show. The contact with air that it creates is crucial to activating and opening up the wine's aromas, like waking up a genie in a bottle. Repeat this process as you please. When it comes to a wine's flavor, aroma delivers the biggest payload, so don't be shy about sniffing.

What are you smelling? Fruit? If so, what kind: red or black; tree fruit or citrus or tropical; fresh or dried? Or are you sensing more earthy flavors, such as vegetables, herbs, or tar? How about something savory, such as coffee grounds, spices, or toast? Maybe there's more minerality— it reminds you of something rock-ish—like wet stone or seashell. (I'll come back to these terms throughout the book, so don't worry if they're not clicking quite yet.)

It's easy to feel overwhelmed when you're hunting for aromas in the glass because the realm of possibilities is so vast—that and you're probably just not used to trying to identify smells on command. Familiarizing yourself with the main categories of wine's aromas and flavors will give you a baseline idea of what to look for. But please, remember that this is a highly personal and subjective game, so don't ever be shy about calling out references that are unique and specific to your taste memories.

Note: *If there are any faults or flaws in the wine, you'll likely pick up on them during this step. So keep a nostril out for any wonky smells, too; e.g., wet dog and cardboard if it's corked.*

Where Do a Wine's Aromas & Flavors Come From?

Wine aromas and flavors can be broken down into three categories: primary, secondary, and tertiary. *Primary* aromas and flavors originate from the grape varietal and the vineyard environment; *secondary* aromas and flavors are a product of what happens during the winemaking process and the winemaker's influence, such as fermentation and aging vessel choices; and *tertiary* aromas and flavors are what develop as a wine ages over time, in a barrel and/or in a bottle.

You can generally expect to find a combination of the categories represented in every glass, but of course the ratio will vary depending on things such as the style and age of the wine. A younger wine will exhibit more primary flavors, whereas an older, oak-aged wine will have you perceiving more secondary and tertiary flavors. The following is not a comprehensive list of every flavor you can find in each aroma/flavor category, but it will give you a jumping-off point! ⟶

PRIMARY AROMAS AND FLAVORS

Fruit

- *Red: Strawberry, Cherry, Raspberry, Cranberry*
- *Black/Blue: Blackberry, Blueberry, Plum, Black Currant*
- *Citrus: Lemon, Lime, Grapefruit, Orange*
- *Orchard/Stone: Apple, Pear, Peach, Nectarine, Apricot*
- *Tropical: Pineapple, Mango, Lychee, Passion Fruit, Melon*

Floral:

- *Rose, Jasmine, Violet, Honeysuckle, Lavender, Chamomile*

Green/Vegetal/Botanical:

- *Herbs, Grass, Tomato, Bell Pepper, Pea, Fennel, Celery, Tea Leaf, Eucalyptus, Beet*

Spice:

- *Cinnamon, Peppercorn, Anise, Clove, Ginger, Cardamom, Saffron, Curry*

Earth:

- *Rock, Seashell, Chalk, Flint, Salt, Potting Soil, Tar, Slate, West Stone, Gravel*

SECONDARY AROMAS AND FLAVORS

- *Microbial: Brioche, Biscuit, Toast, Baked Bread, Cream, Yogurt, Butter, Buttered Popcorn*

- *Oak Aging: Vanilla, Baking Spices, Tobacco, Coconut, Dill*

TERTIARY AROMAS AND FLAVORS

Aging: Dried Fruit, Caramel, Butterscotch, Coffee, Forest Floor, Mushroom, Tobacco, Honey, Nuts, Toast, Petrol, Leather, Truffle, Cured Meat

STEP 3: TASTE IT.

Take a sip. Finally! You've earned it. Give it a little swirl 'n' swish around your mouth while taking in a teeny bit of air—as though you're sucking on an invisible cocktail straw. Doing this helps pull the aromatic compounds into your retronasal passage, allowing the flavors to pop. What are you tasting? Are they the same flavors as you were smelling, or are some new ones peeking through? Does it feel as though there are lots of different flavors to talk about or only a couple? Do they leave a long, lasting impression or disappear quickly?

Aside from flavor, this is also the time to assess the wine's essential components (and there are words associated with all of them, which will come up throughout the book). They include the following.

Acidity

Where does the wine fall on the sourness scale? You'll notice the presence of acid on the sides of your tongue and because your mouth is literally watering.

Tannin

This is the thing (mostly in red wine) that is responsible for that drying-out-of-the-tongue-and-gums sensation. It's also what gives a wine a bitter taste, which you'll notice at the back of your palate.

Alcohol

More than just the thing that makes this a 21+ beverage, it's what gives your wine its body-ody-ody. Lower-alcohol wines will be lighter weight, whereas higher-alcohol wines will feel richer and heavier and can also leave you with a burning-at-the-back-of-your-throat sensation.

Texture

Does it feel lean and chiseled on your palate, or is it more round and fleshy? Or somewhere in between? Or, if it's a sparkling, what are the bubbles like? Pinprick sharp or fatter and frothier?

Sugar

There are sweet wines and dry wines, and wines that fall somewhere in between. Whatever your feelings about each of them are, the fact of the matter is, you cannot make wine without sugar. Sugar (in the form of unfermented grape juice) + yeast = alcohol + CO_2. For the most part, the natural sugar is converted to alcohol through the fermentation process, leaving a dry wine. When some of the sugar is left in and not converted to alcohol, it produces a semisweet or sweet wine. If you taste sweetness, it'll most likely be on the tip of your tongue.

As far as tasting note terms related to these components are concerned, here are a few key ones that have to do with a wine's sugar content.

DRY

This one is easy peasy; it's the wine drinker's way of saying "not sweet."

Get used to using this word a lot. Like, a *lot* a lot. Basically all the time. Because the overwhelming majority of wines—pretty much all reds, and most whites, rosés, and sparklings—are made in a dry style.

Look for clues on the label. Some wines that are commonly made in a range of sweetness levels will note on the label if the wine is made in a dry style. For German Rieslings, look for the word _Trocken_. For a Chenin Blanc from Vouvray in France's Loire Valley, keep an eye out for the word _sec._

Champagne has 'em, too, except, confusingly, dry/_sec_ is _not_ the least sweet style; that is _brut nature._

For still whites and rosés that have no sweetness level designator on the label, here's a relatively fail-safe trick: Check out the alcohol by volume (ABV) percentage. Generally, anything at or above 12 to 12.5 percent will be dry.

OFF DRY

This is how you would describe a wine that *technically* has a little sweetness to it. That is, a little residual sugar was left in the wine instead of being converted into alcohol. Think bittersweet chocolate chips versus unsweetened ones. This applies almost exclusively to white wines, usually in the 7 to 11 percent ABV range. A German Riesling labeled *Kabinett* is a perfect example.

Please, *please*, for the love of all that is good and holy and wine professionals' sanity everywhere, try to hold off from using this word unless you're drinking a legit sweet wine or a dessert wine (more on that on page 30).

Here's the thing, and it is understandably confusing: Just because a wine has the aroma or flavor of something we associate with being sweet—fruit, chocolate, honey, jam—that does not necessarily mean it tastes sweet. That's your brain playing tricks on you (like when it made you think texting your ex after one too many glasses of wine was a good idea). Don't get me wrong; wine can be suuuuper fruity or rich, but if it doesn't have a certain level of residual sugar (18+ g/L), if sweetness isn't hitting the tip of your tongue and lingering after you swallow, it's technically not sweet wine. There are other words for that, including "fruit-forward," "jammy," and "fruit bomb."

Wines That Technically Are Semisweet or Sweet

There are a few ways of making semisweet and sweet wines. The most common is to stop fermentation a bit early in the winemaking process, before the yeast has had a chance to convert most of the sugar into alcohol. This leaves a wine that has some residual sugar left in it; *Kabinett* and *Auslese* Riesling, *demi-sec* Chenin Blanc, *demi-sec* Champagne, and Moscato are great examples.

Wines made by having their fermentation process halted by the addition of a neutral grape spirit are called "fortified wines." Think port, Madeira, and sherry. Adding the spirit increases the alcohol content of the wine, usually to about 17 percent, but *when* it's added determines its final sweetness level.

Another way to go is to make wine from grapes that have naturally high sugar levels; that, for example, are picked later in the harvest so they've started to raisinate or have been infected with the (good!) mold *botrytis*, aka noble rot, which causes grapes to shrivel and their sugar levels to increase. Think Sauternes, Tokaji Aszù, and other wines labeled "late harvest."

When you see any of the following wines in the wild, you can feel confident about commenting on their sweetness.

- Riesling, *specifically* at the *Auslese* or TBA (*Trockenbeerenauslese*) level
- *Demi-sec* Chenin Blanc
- Champagne, *specifically* labeled *demi-sec* or *doux*
- Moscato
- White Zinfandel
- Port
- Madeira
- Sherry, *specifically* cream, Moscatel, and Pedro Ximénez
- Sauternes
- Vin doux naturel
- Tokaji Aszú
- Ice wine

DRINKING GAME ALERT!

Dry vs. Sweet Wine

Pour a glass of a dry, *Trocken* German Riesling and a glass of a sweet, *Auslese* German Riesling. How do the aromas compare to the taste? The fruit aromas might be prominent in both, but on the palate the *Auslese* Riesling actually tastes sweet, like a super ripe piece of fruit, whereas the *Trocken* leans more toward sour citrus flavors. Take a sip of each one alternately. If you take a sip of the sweet one first, followed by a sip of the dry, you should notice that it makes the dry one taste even drier.

STEP 4: WHAT DO YOU THINK?

This is the last step, and it's a short one because it's simple. Whaddya think? You will have the answers here, not I. Did you like it? Want to drink more or buy it again? Yes? No? Why? Why not?

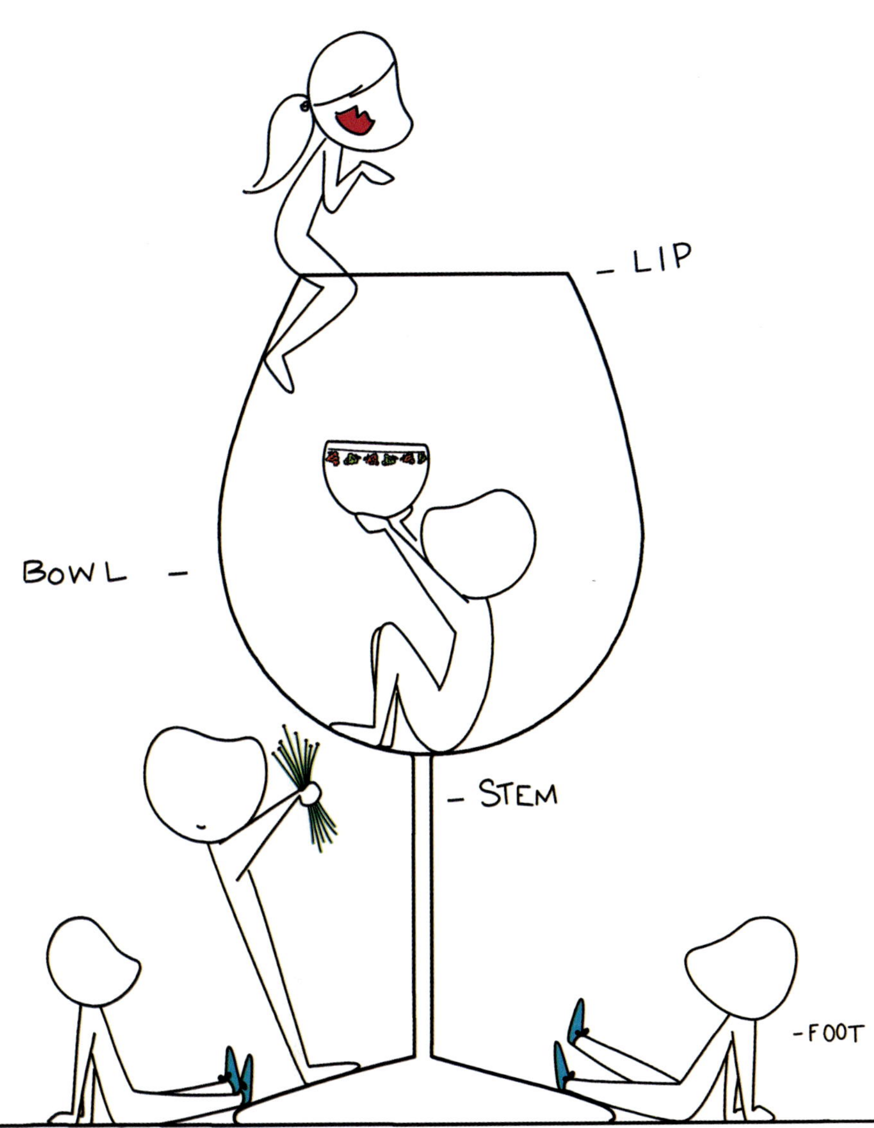

ANATOMY
OF A
WINE
GLASS
- LIP
BOWL -
- STEM
-FOOT

ANATOMY OF A WINE LABEL

Here are a few maybe not so obvious terms for what you see on a wine label.

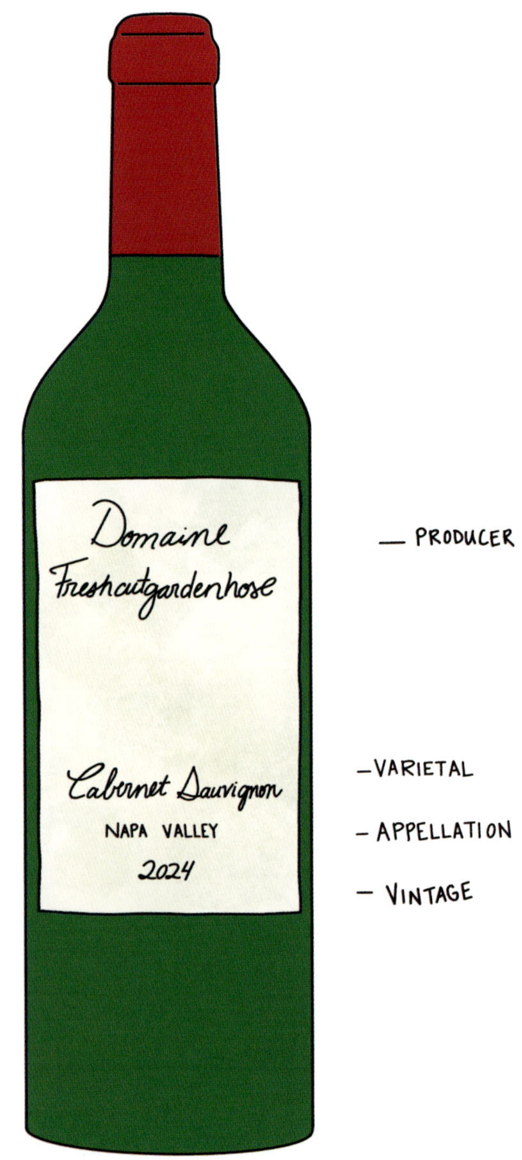

Vintage

This has nothing to do with what's-old-is-new-again finds from yore; it's just the year in which the grapes for the wine were harvested.

Producer

An alternative, more in-the-know way of saying "winery" or "winemaker."

"Have you ever tried wine from this producer? It's new to me, but it came highly recommended by the people at my favorite bottle shop."

Appellation

The name of the geographical location where the grapes for the wine were grown; basically, the wine equivalent of place of birth on a birth certificate. These locations are legally defined and regulated by government agencies to protect and enforce quality standards and can be as broad as a country (e.g., "vin de France") or as specific as a single vineyard.

Varietal

This is a popular, wine-fancy way of saying "type of grape."

It can also be used to describe a wine that is made exclusively (or predominantly) from a single grape variety (Chardonnay, Cabernet Sauvignon, etc.), which, depending on where

the wine is from, may be featured on the
bottle's label.

If you're in a restaurant talking to a sommelier,
reading a wine magazine, or at a good bottle
shop, you might also hear the term "varietally
correct" used to describe a wine. It's a way of
saying that a wine made from a specific grape
tastes like what is stereotypically expected from
that grape, that it has the most classic of flavor
markers—e.g., a New Zealand Sauvignon Blanc
having notes of grapefruit, passionfruit, gooseberry, and grass. In today's wine landscape, you
could argue that the term feels a little dated; it
implies that if a wine doesn't taste like the
so-called classic expression of the grape, it's not
right in some way. But wine is so much more than
a black-and-white game; there's a lot of room for,
and beauty in, coloring outside the lines.

A Basic Guide to Glassware

I'll be honest: I'm really not much of a stickler when it comes to some of the ritualistic aspects of wine service, such as using the "appropriate" glassware for a certain wine. But it's worth mentioning that there is logic (a lot, actually) behind the various wineglass shapes.

Check out this quick primer for an overview of the major wineglass styles:

- *AP glass,* aka all-purpose glass, aka the "If you're only allowed one option, choose this glass" glass. Stemmed with a U-shaped bowl that narrows slightly as it gets up to the top, you can use this super versatile glass for any style of wine.

- *Burgundy bowl,* aka the one with the big, wide bowl. The added aeration provided by the extra space combined with the narrow opening at the lip accentuates the delicate aroma of lighter-bodied reds. It's also a great option for orange wines and fuller-bodied whites.

- *Bordeaux glass,* aka the supersized version of the AP glass, best suited for medium-to-full-bodied reds. The larger bowl helps mellow and smooth out wines that are high octane with rich fruit and big tannins.

- *Flute,* aka the sparkling wine glass. It's distinguished by its small, narrow, long bowl, which encourages the formation of a continuous stream of bubbles. It's great for a celebratory aesthetic, not so great for really appreciating the aroma of a sparkling wine.

- *Dessert glass,* aka copita. The short-stemmed junior version of an AP glass. Use it to drink port, Madeira, sherry, and dessert wines. The smaller bowl helps slow evaporation and concentrates the sweet aromas and flavors that are characteristic of these wines.

2 Pleased to Meet You

First Impressions and Conversation Starters

If you're not in the habit of talking about wine
when you drink it, taster's block can be real.
Maybe this sounds familiar: OMG, how do I kick
it off? Or convey an overall initial assessment?
Am I just supposed to start listing flavors? Or are
there some classic opening lines I should be using?
Is there a better, more sophisticated way of saying
"It smells like *x*"? There's gotta be. Help!

Take a deep breath. The words and expressions
in this section have you covered.

OPENS
WITH

What flavors is the wine using to start the conversation? It's as though you're at a speed date mixer . . . wait, is that still a thing? Scratch that. So you both swiped right. Yay! What line is the wine leading with in the DMs to get your attention?

"Opens with seductive aromas of dark cherry, truffle, and roses—swoon."

You've invited your wine over for dinner (or lunch? brunch? mid-afternoon aperitif?... we don't judge). What's it handing you in the welcome basket when you open the door?

GREETS
YOU WITH

"This Sauv Blanc immediately greets you with its signature green profile: fresh-cut grass, bell pepper, lime, melon, and gooseberry."

OFFERS
UP

"Greets you with" but, like, sexier. You are on the throne, and the wine, your subject, is before you on bended knee. Behold what it is presenting for your consideration, pleasure, and enjoyment.

"I love the green profile that this Sauv Blanc offers up: fresh-cut grass, bell pepper, lime, melon, and gooseberry. Super classic."

"Greets you with," but slightly aggro.

HITS YOU
IN THE
FACE WITH

"The fresh-cut grass, bell pepper, lime, melon, and gooseberry immediately hit you in the face—exactly what I expect from Sauvignon Blanc."

OUT OF THE GATE

Once you've swirled and sniffed, it's off to the races! What's taking the lead in these first few moments of tasting? Similarly to "Opens with" and its synonyms, you can list some specific flavors with this one, such as a particular fruit or herb. But this phrase lets you take it one step further if you want to. It can precede an initial general impression of the wine (e.g., super aromatic, decadent) and/or its personality (e.g., shy, friendly).

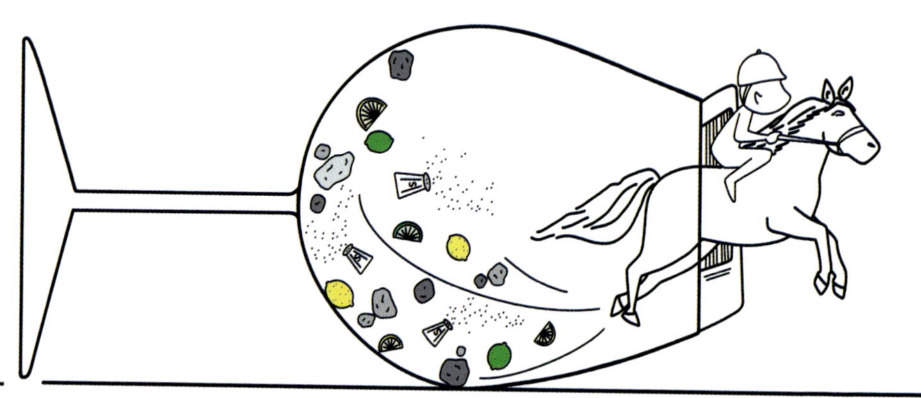

"Super vibrant with tons of energy out of the gate, kicking up a tornado of salty citrus and rocks."

The pitch is right down the middle. *Swoosh, crack* goes the bat. Quick, rattle off your immediate first impressions about what the wine is launching at you!

"A little shy off the bat, but after a couple swirls, blackberry and baking spices start to peek through."

BURSTING
WITH

When a wine has so much of a given flavor(s) that it feels as though it cannot be contained; like a *really* juicy piece of gossip. Or the five extra outfits that are keeping your suitcase from closing but that you need—*need*—to take with you on vacation. (Even though you probably won't wear any of them.) Use this to describe the flavors that feel can't-miss obvious to you. Often paired with descriptions of fruit—maybe because fruit is juicy and "burst" evokes a liquidy kind of visual? Just a totally unfounded personal theory—but can also describe a more general character, such as acidity or minerality.

"Right out of the gate, absolutely bursting with red fruit, black pepper, licorice, lemon zest, and bunches of wild herbs and purple flowers."

This is just another way of saying "a lot." Yup, like the slang term you already know and love and use. Simple. Easy. Boom.

IT'S GOT X FOR DAYS

"Right off the bat, it's got red fruit and smoke for daaaaays."

HINT [OR WHISPER] OF

Not every flavor is in the front row under the spotlight, giving you "Pay attention to me!" jazz hands. Use this when identifying more demure, less showboaty supporting character flavors, the ones you just barely taste and catch only fleeting whiffs of.

"Love the hint of red fruit and smoke on the finish."

This is sommelier code for "smells like" and/or "tastes like." Typically, you'll use this to precede a listicle-style, CliffsNotes-esque summary of the aromas and flavors you're picking up on in a wine. It can be used at any point in a description, but if you don't know where to start with your tasting note, this is an easy go-to. Try partnering it with "opens with" and co. early on in a description.

NOTES OF

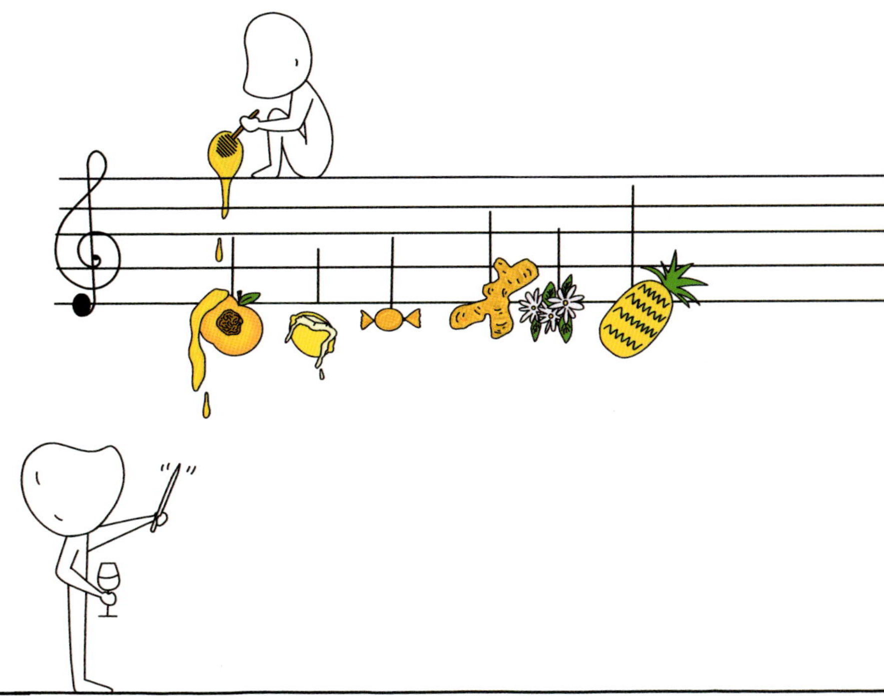

"Greets you with notes of honey-drenched apricot, lemon butter, caramel, ginger, honeysuckle, and ripe pineapple."

LONG/ LENGTH

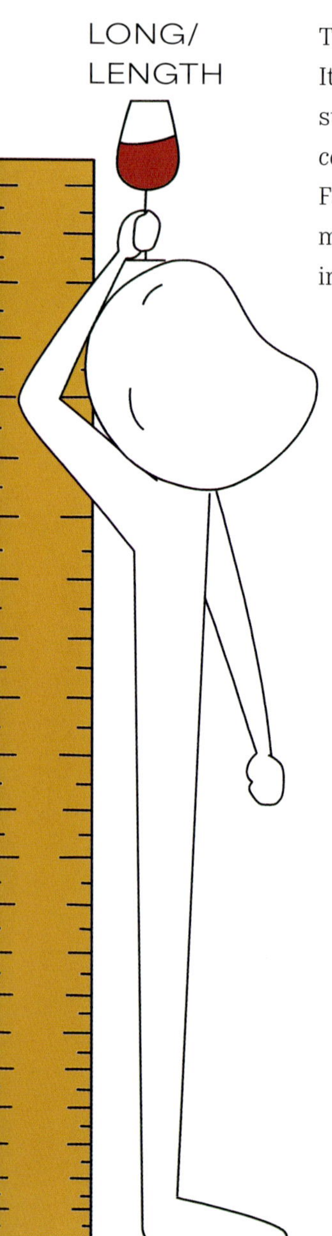

This is a qualitative assessment of a wine's finish. It's how you would describe a wine whose flavor stays with you, like the *Holy-sh*t-didn't-see-that-coming* ending of an epic true crime podcast. Fascinating. Intriguing. You can't get it off your mind. It just … lingers … It's a compliment; an indicator of a well-made wine with complexity.

"Amazingly long finish. Seriously, those notes of cherry and black pepper are not letting go (and I am not mad at it)."

SHORT

Like when that series you just started getting into isn't renewed for season two and you're left in "will they/won't they" cliffhanger purgatory. The fun is over before it had a chance to get started. Basically, it's how you would describe a wine whose flavor is lacking, shall we say, stamina. Maybe it piques your interest with a couple of notes at first, but then it drops off anticlimactically. Womp, womp.

"Bummer, the finish feels a bit short—the fruit just kind of disappears abruptly."

On the [Nose, Palate, Front, Back, Finish]

An "on the" reference helps you be more specific about *where* you're picking up what you're picking up on in the wine. Is it something you're smelling? Tasting? A lasting impression? Identifying these distinctions will not only make the description more complete and effective when discussing the wine with others, but it will help you slow down and really think about the wine you're drinking.

While it is pretty ubiquitous in an educational or professional context, if saying stuff such as "Picking up notes of *x* on the palate" feels a little too highfalutin and try-hard-y for you, maybe go with a cooler, more casual Gen Z version like "The [nose/palate/front/back/finish] is giving . . ."?

Nose: Aroma, a flavor you sense when you smell the wine

Palate: Taste, a flavor you get when you take a sip of and drink the wine

Front: Something you taste at the front of your palate, the tip of your tongue; could also be used to describe the flavors you notice first

Back: Something you taste more at the back of your palate and throat after swallowing

Finish: Last impression, the flavor that lingers at the end, longer than the rest

This is a way of saying "version of" or "presentation of." It's frequently used when comparing two (or more) wines with each other, usually made from the same varietal but maybe coming from different winegrowing regions (see some examples below) or different producers within a similar area who have varying stylistic tendencies.

Same Grape, Different Regional Expression

- **Pinot Grigio:** *Italy (Veneto, Alto Adige, Friuli) vs. Oregon vs. Alsace, France*
- **Sauvignon Blanc:** *Sancerre, France, vs. Marlborough, New Zealand, vs. California*
- **Chenin Blanc:** *Loire Valley, France, vs. South Africa*
- **Riesling:** *Germany vs. Austria vs. Alsace, France, vs. New York*
- **Chardonnay:** *California (Sonoma, Napa) vs. Burgundy, France*
- **Pinot Noir:** *California vs. Oregon; California or Oregon vs. Burgundy, France*
- **Malbec:** *Mendoza, Argentina, vs. Loire Valley or Cahors, France*
- **Syrah:** *Rhône Valley, France, vs. Barossa Valley, Australia*
- **Zinfandel:** *California vs. Puglia, Italy (where it is known as Primitivo)*
- **Cabernet Sauvignon:** *California or Washington vs. Bordeaux, France*

"This producer's expression of Riesling has always been a personal favorite; such an incredible combination of richness and finesse."

It's an Old World/New World After All

"Old World" and "New World" are terms used to identify and broadly categorize a wine and its style based on its geographical growing region.

"Old World" refers to the OG winemaking regions of Europe, the Middle East, and North Africa: Think France, Italy, Spain, Portugal, Germany, Austria, Switzerland, Georgia, Hungary, Croatia, Lebanon, Morocco, and Israel. "New World" basically includes everyone else: North and South America, Australia, New Zealand, and South Africa (to name the big ones).

Don't expect to encounter the designations all that often in your day-to-day wine-drinking adventures, but you might come across them in a publication or on a restaurant wine list or in a bottle shop for organizational purposes, although even among the professional community, the terms are increasingly considered to be archaic.

Still, they can be helpful as an indicator of the broad characteristics you can expect from a wine or used as a reference point when comparing bottles or talking about a particular winemaker's style. For example, "I think you might like this California Chardonnay. This producer makes wines in more of an Old World style. It's definitely not a buttery oak bomb."

Stereotypically, Old World wines tend to be lighter in body and alcohol, with higher acidity, earthiness, and minerality (more on these words later). New World wines are typically more on the fuller-bodied, higher-alcohol side, with richer, riper fruit flavors. Of course, if you remember only one thing about wine, it's that it pretty much always operates in gray areas. So don't take these as hard-and-fast definitions. That would be too easy. And we all know that wine has a damn hard time being easy.

Use this to describe what you identify to be a dominant characteristic in the wine. Who's behind the wheel on this vinous joyride? The fruit? The acidity? The minerality? Whatever it is, it's no passenger princess. Particularly when used with "acid" and "fruit," it's a bit of a softer, more delicate way of expressing something that could be taken the wrong way. For example, instead of saying "tart AF," which could be 100 percent correct but also put some people off, you say "acid-driven." Instead of saying "Oh wow, this tastes really fruity" or, god forbid, "sweet," you say it's "fruit-driven" to indicate the fruit flavors are really poppin'.

[MINERAL, ACID, FRUIT]-DRIVEN

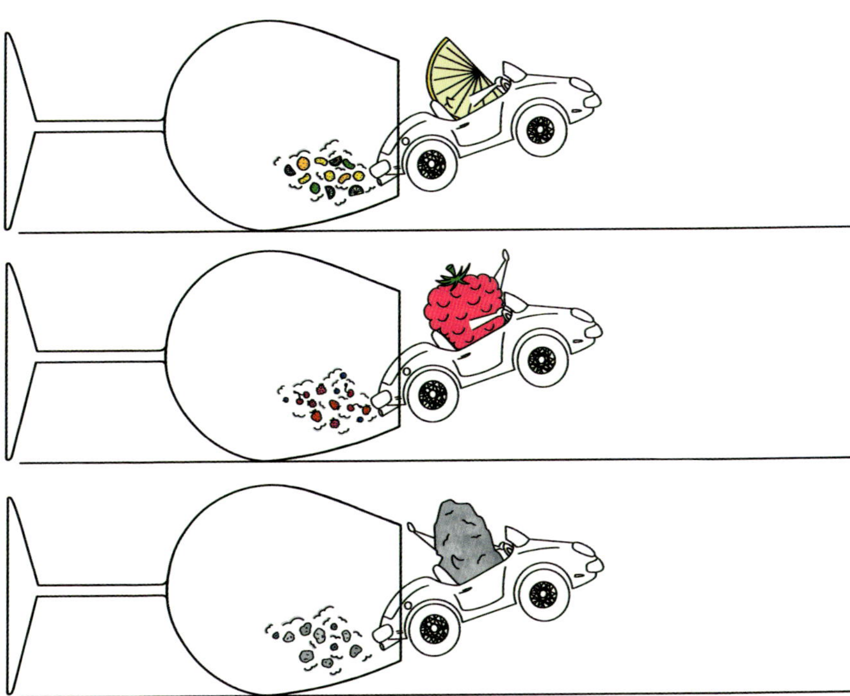

"This Albariño tastes like we're licking rocks from a beach by the ocean, super saline and mineral driven!"

BALANCED

When a wine has that "juuuuuust right" thing Goldilocks was searching for in the three bears' house. Used to describe an overall impression of a wine whose various components—flavor concentration, acidity, texture, alcohol level, and so on—are well matched, playing together harmoniously. You're not noticing too much of this or too little of that. Along with calling a wine "complex," it's one of the, if not *the*, ultimate compliments you can give a wine, something all good wines strive to be.

"Super impressed with the balance in this wine—the way the laser-like acidity and mineral edge in the texture match up with that bright, generous fruit profile … obsessed."

Used as a general assessment, it's some of the highest praise you can bestow upon a wine. A wine is complex when it gives you a lot to think about and talk about and describe. It has depth and length. It has character. Its textures, flavors, and components are multifaceted yet balanced. It evolves as you enjoy it, so you pick up on new things as you continue to sip and sniff. It's not just *"Oh, yeah, it's nice and light and smells like cherries."* It's *"Oh, wow! Bursting with bright sour cherry, red currant, and underripe raspberry. Then come these whispers of freshly brewed espresso and bitter dark chocolate, plus something reminiscent of what it smells like walking through the forest after a rain shower. And it just glides across the palate, the tannins are super elegant."* And, and, and. The way you might talk about a Michelangelo fresco versus your kid's fingerpainting. (Sorry, I'm sure they're a genius, but you get the point.)

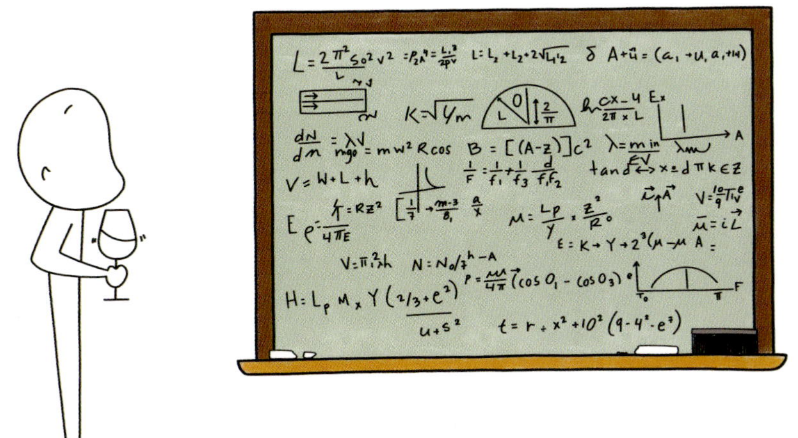

3

The Nose Knows

Talking About Aroma

The wisecracking, immature twenty-one-year-old who still lives inside me wants to be like "Obviously, *taste* is the best, most enjoyable part about drinking wine. *Duh.*" But the truth of the matter is, the real MVP of the wine tasting experience belongs to smell. Something like 80 percent of what we "taste" in wine, the flavors we experience, is picked up through smell. Seriously, try pinching your nose while you take a sip of wine. Sure, you'll be able to notice things such as whether it has high acidity (because your mouth will be watering) or aspects of its texture (such as your mouth feeling dried out because it has a lot of tannin). But without your sense of smell, you won't be getting much of anything in the flavor department.

That's why aroma is so important. So important, in fact, that wine peeps have even developed a whole set of words and expressions—not about specific flavors (they're important, too, but we'll get to those in the next chapter) but that help set up a conversation about a wine's aroma. And that's what the following pages are all about.

BOUQUET/ BOUQUET OF

A synonym for aroma or fragrance that can be used in place of "nose/on the nose/nose of." A traditionalist would tell you that the term should *technically* be reserved for describing scents that come from the winemaking or aging process (aka the secondary and tertiary aromas), such as buttery and baking spices. But realistically speaking, no one's going to rake you over the coals if you use it to describe the curious and captivating smells that can show up in wine: florals and wild herbs, cured meats, fruit, a freshly brewed cup of tea, tennis balls, honey, sweet cream, pencil shavings … eat your heart out, Edible Arrangements.

"Opens up with a captivating bouquet of dark roast coffee, mushroom, cinnamon, and toasted almond. Then some notes of wild herbs, fig, cigar smoke, and rocks come through on the finish."

Like "bouquet," you can use this as a more eloquent sub for "smells like." When taking a sniff of your wine feels like visiting a department store fragrance counter (but with a *much* more diverse range of scents being spritzed in your face).

PERFUME/ PERFUME OF

"Ooooh! Loving the perfume coming off this Chianti! A little roasted tomato and oregano, with hints of sour cherry and balsamic."

HUGE NOSE

Maybe *you* wouldn't take it as a compliment, but when it comes to wine, having a big ol' schnoz is very much a desirable quality. It's a way of saying that the wine is highly aromatic. And since aroma is such a big part of how we taste and process flavor, for a wine to have a huge nose is considered to be a huge positive.

"The nose on this Torrontés is huge! I feel like I've been dropped into the middle of a blossoming garden orchard, surrounded by peaches, lemons, jasmine, and roses."

When it feels as though the volume of the wine's aroma has been cranked up to the max, bass thumping through the speakers. You can't ignore it; it has your attention.

"I love how loud the nose on this is, all those intense aromas of pear, ginger, peach, jasmine, and honey are cranked up to the max."

JUMPING [LEAPING, SOARING] OUT OF THE GLASS

When the aroma is so big and so intense it feels as though it's making a jailbreak. The wine has been poured, it has been set *free*, and it's heading straight for your nose.

"Have you smelled the Syrah yet? Super classic, with notes of savory bacon fat, black pepper, and leather leaping out of the glass."

Picture Wile E. Coyote rigging a bunch of TNT to your glass. You swirl, you go in for your sniff, and then *boom*, gotcha! Aromas blast right up into your nostrils.

EXPLOSIVE

"The nose on this Malvasia is absolutely explosive! It feels like a bomb of wild white flowers and citrus just went off in my nose—so freaking pretty."

WAFTS UP FROM THE GLASS

Like "jumps/leaps/soars" but with slightly less intensity. You notice the aromas, but the energy is much more chill and laid-back: come-hither eyes versus hands waving "Look at me! Look at me! Look at me!"

"Delicate notes of citrus, toasted almond, brioche, and herbs waft up from the glass."

Wines We'd Totally Wear as Perfume

If you like wines with big, loud leaping-out-of-the-glass noses, be sure to check out wines made from these highly aromatic grapes:

White: Riesling, Gewürztraminer, Muscat, Torrontés, Viognier, Malvasia, Moschofilero, Kerner

Red: Pinot Noir, Cinsault, Freisa, Grignolino, Schiava, Grenache, Syrah, Nebbiolo

DRINKING GAME ALERT!

Low-Aromatic vs. Highly Aromatic Wine

Try a glass of Pinot Grigio or Pinot Blanc, both of which are pretty softly aromatic, next to a glass of Gewürztraminer or Torrontés, which are both highly aromatic. What do you notice about the levels of aroma intensity in both? Observe how the nose on the Pinot Grigio or Pinot Blanc is quieter and more subdued than that of the other, which is stronger and louder. Do you see how the Gewürztraminer or Torrontés smells as though it could be bottled and sold as a perfume?

QUIET

How you would characterize a wine that is lacking aromatic intensity. When it feels as though the wine has something to share but it's holding back, keeping its thoughts and opinions to itself. Not all wines are equally aromatic; as I said before, some grapes are naturally more so than others. And admittedly, because it's not an even playing field, it can make giving this kind of assessment a bit tricky. But generally, if you say that a wine is "quiet," you're expressing disappointment in its aromatic intensity. You're saying that you expected, and wish, that it had more going on in that department.

"The nose on this one feels a little quiet; I'm not getting much out of the gate. Maybe it just needs some time to breathe."

When there's wine in the glass but it's giving your
nose the silent treatment. A more severe version
of "quiet." Could be caused by a flaw in the wine,
such as cork taint.

MUTED

"Oof, that's disappointing—the nose is completely muted. Hardly any aroma
coming through."

4 Take Me to Flavortown

Talking About Fruit, Rocks, and Everything in Between

When you come to the point in the tasting when it's time to start identifying a wine's specific flavors, it's easy to feel intimidated, especially if you're not used to focusing on how the things in your world smell and taste. Wine people like to do this: catch, collect, and catalog taste memories as though they're playing Pokémon Go: Wine Edition.

It takes practice. And if you really want to get into wine and get better at tasting, it's a worthwhile exercise. The next time you're making bread, for example, take a couple seconds to take in what that yeasty dough smells like. Think about it. File it away in your mind. Go to the farmers' market, buy a bunch of different fruit, and sample them; try to focus on how cherries taste different from strawberries and how the taste of those red fruits varies from that of blackberries or plums. Go through your spice cabinet and smell each container so that differentiating cinnamon from cardamom from allspice becomes second nature to you.

This extends beyond food-related smells and tastes. Find yourself on a farm? Clock those hay, manure, and saddle leather aromas. Visit a garden or florist, and appreciate how the smell of one flower varies from another. You get the idea.

This section won't cover every taste and smell you could possibly call out when describing a wine. That would be a challenge—there's, like, a thousand of them—not to mention the whole spectrum of smell and taste memories that are specific to you. But it's a good start. You'll find some words to use when a wine tastes really fruity and some for when it's not. We'll dig into the rocky concept of minerality and touch on the topic of oak and other fermentation and aging vessels, exploring the impact they have on flavor.

Use this when you want a fun, easy way to synthesize your overall impression of a wine based on two dominant flavors. This is particularly effective when the "parents" are from different flavor categories, such as fruit and mineral, or something floral and something you'd find in your spice cabinet; the odder the couple, the better. And please don't ever be afraid to call out references that are personal to you. If the wine tastes as though your grandma's signature blueberry pie had a baby with the stables at the farm you visited last week—say it!

X AND Y
HAD A
BABY

"Tastes like a freshly shucked oyster and Meyer lemon had a baby."

LIKE A LOVE CHILD BETWEEN X AND Y

Like "X and Y had a baby" but with a bit of dramatic flair.

"Oh, hell, yes, it's like a love child between gasoline and a tart green apple!"

Yes, wine people use "juicy" as a way to describe fermented grape juice. Take it in. Accept it. Use it when you think the wine has a succulent, mouthwatering kind of quality. It could apply to a red or white, but usually to a younger wine with fresh, ripe, fruit-forward aromas and flavors matched with bright acidity. It's the kind of wine that goes down easy, as if you were sucking it out of a juice box with a straw, elementary-school-lunch-style.

"This Beaujolais is super juicy! It's legit giving me strawberry Gushers vibes, and I mean that in the best possible way."

FRUIT FORWARD

How you would describe a wine that is technically dry but has really prominent fruit flavors. Like, the fruit is coming on to you *strong*. If you met it at a bar, it'd be complimenting your outfit, buying you another round, and making sure to get your number before the end of the night. Though its fruitiness is dominant, overall the wine still feels pretty balanced. Generally, this is more of a neutral observation, but whether you enjoy it or not depends on your personal taste.

"California Zinfandel is one of my favorite fruit-forward reds—always tons of rich, concentrated red and black berry flavors on the palate."

When it feels as though the richness and intensity of the fruit flavor have been raised to the power of ten. Think about the difference between drip coffee and cold brew—thin, weak, and watery vs. bold, rich, and extracted. This is usually used to describe fuller-bodied, fruit-forward reds but could also be applied to some heavier, lusher styles of white.

CONCENTRATED

"Out of the gate, the Grenache is offering up some really intense notes of concentrated strawberry and black cherry."

JAMMY

A cousin of "fruit forward" used to describe red wines with a fruit flavor (usually red and black fruits such as berries, cherries, figs, and plums) that has what you might describe as a cooked sweetness and a thicker texture. Think about the difference in flavor and texture between a fresh strawberry and the strawberry jam you slather onto your PB&J. One's lighter and more vibrant; the other, more concentrated and richer. Some wine people can be a little turn-your-nose-up snooty about the term and the wines associated with it, probably because it became so ubiquitous and overused, like "smooth." But hey, if wines with jammy fruit notes speak to you and you want to talk about them, great! Like what you like; you do you. Australian Shiraz, California Zinfandel, Argentinian Malbec, and Grenache-based blends from France's southern Rhône Valley are good places to look for examples of this.

"If you're looking for a fruit-forward red, I would go with the Shiraz. Very rich and jammy with notes of blackberry and plum, but it also has a nice hint of black pepper spice on the finish."

"Fruit forward" but taken to the extreme. Like, way over the top. Gone too far. When the fruit flavor is so intense, so ripe, so concentrated that it basically blows out your palate. It's the only thing about the wine you can really taste, dominating every other flavor and overpowering other key structural elements, such as acidity and tannin. It's most often associated with red wines, frequently from New World regions, that are higher in alcohol and low in tannin and acidity. Generally used as a dig, because you're basically saying that the wine is not balanced.

"That wine is a total fruit bomb, like a bunch of overripe berries just exploded on my tongue."

SAVORY

A catchall term for any nonfruity flavors you might pick up on, such as tomato (yes, I know it's *technically* a fruit, but you know what I mean), olive, mushroom, and bell pepper. Herbs and spices such as black pepper, rosemary, saffron, and ginger fall into the savory bucket, too, as do flavors such as minerals (think salt and rocks), smoked meat, leather, tea, and tobacco. If you're seeking savory in your wine: For red, try Syrah, Mourvèdre, and Cabernet Franc from France; Sangiovese, Nebbiolo, and Aglianico from Italy; Tempranillo and Carignan (aka Cariñena) from Spain. For whites, check out Grüner Veltliner from Austria; dry Chenin Blanc and Savagnin from France; Assyrtiko from Greece; Albariño and White Rioja from Spain.

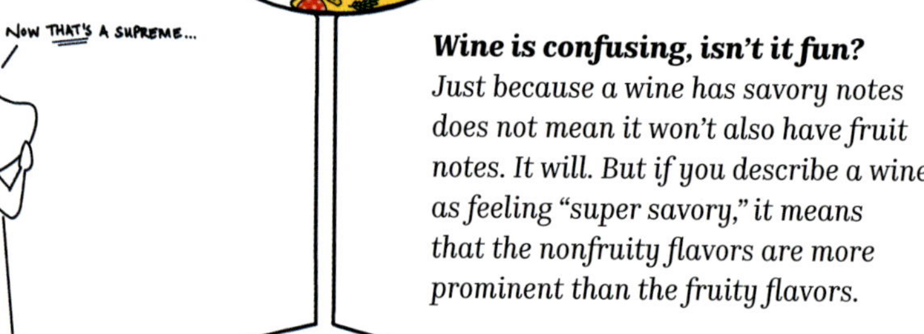

Wine is confusing, isn't it fun?
Just because a wine has savory notes does not mean it won't also have fruit notes. It will. But if you describe a wine as feeling "super savory," it means that the nonfruity flavors are more prominent than the fruity flavors.

"I don't drink Mourvèdre all that often. I forgot how savory it is! That 'gamy, roasted meat encrusted with wild herbs' thing hits you right in the face."

The Difference Terroir Makes

Set up a flight of three wines: Pinot Grigio from Italy, Pinot Gris from Oregon, and Pinot Gris from Alsace. Same grape, each from a different region. Swirl, sniff, and taste. What differences are you picking up on among them? See how the Italian leans more mineral and the Alsatian more fruit forward? And what do you think about the one from Oregon; how does that compare? Once you've tried that flight, play again with a Chenin Blanc from the Loire and one from South Africa. Or if you're more of a red wine drinker, try a Malbec from Argentina side by side with one from southwest France's Cahors region. If you like lush, concentrated berry flavors, the Argentinian expression will be for you. If you're into more of a rustic, earthy, tannic vibe, the French will probably get your vote.

Fruit-Forward vs. Savory, Earthy Wine

In the corner for fruit forward, we have a California Zinfandel; and, representing earthy, a Cabernet Franc from France's Loire Valley (look for the appellation "Saumur" or "Bourgeuil" on the label). Notice how when you smell each of them, the prominent flavors in the Zin are fruit (blackberry, blueberry, strawberry), but in the Cab Franc, vegetal (hello, green bell pepper!) and gravel notes take center stage. When you taste, do you find that the palate follows (matches) the nose? Does the fruit in the Zin taste richer, almost jamlike, whereas the fruit in the Cab Franc leans more tart? Do you still pick up on the mineral and savory notes in the Cab Franc as you drink it?

LANOLIN

In winespeak, this is how you would say "This smells like wax and wet wool." Dead serious. Just a white wine thing, most notably in Chenin Blancs, especially from the Loire Valley, as well as whites made from Sémillon, Viognier, and Viura (the grape used to make whites from Rioja). And get this: It's not used as a diss. That's right, this is a quality that is *appreciated*. It's credited as helping add that little je ne sais quoi to the complexity of the wine's profile, an elusive but intriguing savory note in the aroma that you maybe can't quite put your finger on but that keeps you coming back for more. Sounds weird, I'll admit it, but don't knock it till you've tried it.

"The hint of lanolin on the nose is a dead giveaway that this is a Loire Valley Chenin Blanc, especially combined with the note of honeyed baked apple and that waxy texture on the palate."

EARTHY

A subset of "savory" that is dedicated to a broad range of nonfruit aromas and flavors that remind you of anything from the ground; your "Thank you, Mother Earth, for your beautiful bounty," "Let's forest bathe and be one with nature" flavors. If you want to use it as a more general, broad-strokes descriptor, just say "earthy." But if you want to get more precise about it, go ahead and call out specific subcategories (e.g., vegetal, mineral) or flavor cues, things such as potting soil, wet clay, tar, gravel, hay, barnyard, petrichor, garrigue, forest floor, mushrooms, beets, graphite, and charcoal.

"Earthy notes of tar, dried thyme, wild roses, and black truffle waft up from the glass of this young Nebbiolo."

FOREST FLOOR

Ready for a softball? This just means that the wine's aroma and flavor profile reminds you of what you'd find on the ground if you were walking through a, well, forest. Things such as decaying leaves, soil, rocks, mushrooms, grass, moss, miscellaneous vegetation ... A red wine descriptor, it is most commonly associated with Pinot Noir (especially from Burgundy), but can also be found in Italian Sangiovese and Nebbiolo as well as Bordeaux. It is typically an aroma that develops as a wine ages, so look for it in older vintage bottles.

P.S. If you want to sound extra fancy, you can say *sous bois* (soo bwah), which is the French term for it and literally translates as "under wood."

"The play between tart vibrant red fruit and moody, earthy, forest floor aromas is one of my favorite things about Pinot Noirs from Burgundy."

Digging into Minerality

Here's the tea on minerality: Everyone uses the word, yet no one really agrees on how to define it, how a wine comes to possess it, or if it even exists at all.

Science tells us that no direct link has been found between the minerals in the ground of the vineyard where the grapes are grown and the wine in your glass. But dammit if a glass of Chablis from Burgundy doesn't bring seashells and chalk to mind, or if a Nerello Mascalese from Mount Etna in Sicily doesn't give off a smoky, charred volcanic rock vibe. Maybe it's projection, because those things are part of the makeup of the soil where the wines are produced. Part of the *terroir.** Or maybe it isn't. I say, when you're tasting it in the wine, regardless of why or how it got there, it's real to you.

What you need to know is that when wine people use the word "minerality," they're basically saying that something in the wine reminds them of rocks or rock derivatives in some way. A specific subset of "earthy," it can present as an aroma, a flavor, and/or even a texture. You're most likely to find it in wines that come from cool-climate regions—frequently Old World (Europe, mostly), but also New World places such as Marlborough, New Zealand; Willamette Valley, Oregon; and Chile's Casablanca Valley. Don't expect to pick up on it in wines that are fermented and/or aged in new oak because of the flavors that process imparts (more on that on page 100). And in a description, it's used either matter-of-factly or with a positive connotation. ⟶

---

* The quick-and-dirty download on *terroir.* It's a French term that encapsulates everything about the environment where a grape is grown—the soil, the climate, the elevation of the vineyard, and so on—and the impact it has on the wine produced from it. It's basically the "nature" in the nature versus nurture of how a wine is raised and made.

Minerality is a blanket term, but if you want to get more specific about it, dig into the mine. You'll find some of the most common mineral flavors and the wines they're often associated with.

Flint

- *Sauvignon Blanc (spec. Sancerre, Pouilly-Fumé)*
- *Chardonnay (spec. Chablis)*
- *Assyrtiko*
- *Carricante (spec. Etna Bianco)*
- *Grüner Veltliner*

Chalk

- *Chardonnay (spec. Chablis)*
- *Champagne & English Sparkling*
- *Albariño*
- *Grüner Veltliner*

Limestone

- *Chardonnay (spec. Chablis + Jura)*
- *Champagne*
- *Viura (spec. Rioja)*
- *Savagnin (spec. Jura)*
- *Riesling*

Saline

- *Albariño*
- *Assyrtiko*
- *Vermentino (spec. Corsica)*
- *Verdicchio*
- *Picpoul de Pinet*
- *Melon de Bourgogne (spec. Muscadet)*
- *Sauvignon Blanc*
- *Txakolina*

Petrol

- *Riesling*

Slate

- *Riesling*
- *Garnacha (spec. Priorat)*

Gravel

- *Cabernet Sauvignon
  (spec. Bordeaux; Napa; Coonawarra, Aus)*
- *Sauvignon Blanc + Sémillon
  (spec. Bordeaux)*

Volcanic Rock

- *Nerello Mascalese (spec. Etna Rosso)*
- *Carricante (spec. Etna Bianco)*
- *Assyrtiko (spec. Santorini)*
- *Canary Islands reds + whites*
- *Aglianico*
- *Garganega (spec. Soave)*

Wet Rock

- *Vermentino*
- *Chardonnay (spec. Chablis)*
- *Sauvignon Blanc
  (spec. Sancerre + Pouilly-Fumé)*
- *Albariño*
- *Grüner Veltliner*

Seashell

- *Chardonnay (spec. Chablis)*
- *Melon de Bourgogne (spec. Muscadet)*
- *Albariño*

Tar

- *Nebbiolo (spec. Barolo + Barbaresco)*
- *Syrah (spec. N. Rhône)*
- *Aglianico*

Baked Rock

- *Grenache / Garnacha
  (spec. Châteauneuf-du-Pape, Priorat)*
- *Mourvèdre (spec. Bandol)*
- *Touriga Nacional (spec. Douro)*

GARRIGUE   The not-so-pretty-sounding name—it's pronounced "gah-*reeg*"—for the *very* specific aroma of smoky-peppery wild Mediterranean herbs and shrubs. Think rosemary, sage, thyme, lavender, mint, and juniper. It's most commonly identified as a tasting note in wines from the southwest of France (southern Rhône, Provence, Languedoc), which makes sense given that those plants grow around the vineyards producing the wines from those regions. As I was saying, *terroir*. The aroma also pops up in wines from other Mediterranean regions such as Corsica, Sicily, and Croatia.

"The distinctive aroma of garrigue in this Grenache-Syrah-Mourvèdre blend from the Côtes du Rhône takes me straight back to our vacation there last summer."

PETRICHOR

Pronounced "*peh*-tree-kor," it's *not* the name of a professor from *Harry Potter* but a word used to describe a smell reminiscent of being outside after a rain shower in the middle of a hot, dry summer. Sure, it's a little precious. And definitely specific. But it *is* evocative, isn't it? You could use more words to get your point across—damp soil and foliage, dewy grass, wet gravelly dirt road— but if you want to be efficient, "petrichor" it is. It's definitely more of a flex than a casual conversation kind of term. It can be found in both white and red wines.

"Are you getting that note of petrichor on the Etna Bianco, too? Basically what I would imagine it smells like standing on volcanic rock after a light summer shower."

PYRAZINE

Pronounced "*pee*-rah-zeen," it's the name of the organic compounds responsible for the green herb and vegetal aromas in wine. These compounds exist in all grapes, but they're more noticeable in those that naturally have higher levels of them. They're the reason why your Sauvignon Blanc smells like grass and asparagus and your Cabernet Franc smells like green bell pepper and green beans. Other grapes known for having high levels of pyrazines include Cabernet Sauvignon, Merlot, Malbec, Carménère, and Grüner Veltliner. Use this word only if you really feel like flashing your wine snob card. Otherwise, calling out whatever specific herb and/or veggie aromas you're smelling will do just fine.

"*As expected, there are some super pronounced pyrazine notes in this Saumur Cab Franc—the fresh green bell pepper–jalapeño aroma hits you in the face right out of the gate.*"

GREEN GUIDE

Prep yourself to talk pyrazine by getting to know some of the green flavors you can encounter in various grapes.

Sauvignon Blanc

- *Bell pepper*
- *Grass*
- *Jalapeño*
- *Tarragon*
- *Basil*
- *Snap pea*
- *Asparagus*

Grüner Veltliner

- *Green bean + snap pea*
- *Arugula*
- *Celery*
- *Fava bean*
- *Radish leaf*

Cabernet Franc

- *Bell pepper*
- *Green peppercorn*
- *Jalapeño*
- *Tobacco leaf*
- *Thyme + oregano*

Carménère

- *Bell pepper*
- *Jalapeño + chili pepper*
- *Tomato leaf*

Cabernet Sauvignon

- *Bell pepper*
- *Green peppercorn*
- *Eucalyptus*

Merlot

- *Bell pepper*
- *Tomato leaf*
- *Green olive*

OAKY

Ironically, *not* used to convey that your wine smells like wood but that it smells as though it had a … dalliance? entanglement? special rendezvous? with wood—most likely new oak barrels—at some point in its life at the winery. Let's just say it's not the kind of affair that flies under the radar. Notes such as vanilla, baking spices, butterscotch, caramel, coconut, dill, toast, cigar box, smoke, and toasted nuts are going to be a dead giveaway.

It can be used in reference to white or red wine. Chardonnay from Napa and Sonoma Valley in California is the classic example for white, but white Rioja and whites from Bordeaux also come to mind. And for red, think Tempranillo from Rioja, Napa Valley Cabernet Sauvignon, Australian Shiraz, and Argentinian Malbec. As a tasting note, it can be either a compliment or an insult; as ever, it depends on your preferences.

"I don't know that I'd call this Rioja 'oaky,' but it's definitely got the signature coconut-dill thing on the nose from being aged in American oak."

"Whenever someone tells me they like an 'oaky white,' I always immediately think of California Chardonnay, even though I know a lot of newer producers are moving away from that aged-in-new-oak style."

Caramel

BUTTERY

The 1980s called, and they want their Chardonnay description back. Okay, sorry, that was shady. But that *is* about the time we all became conditioned like Pavlov's dogs to associate that flavor with that varietal, even though Chardonnay is not innately buttery. Flavorwise, it's actually a pretty neutral grape, a blank canvas, which is why so many winemakers love it.

That rich, unctuous note of movie theater popcorn butter in your wine is actually malolactic fermentation at play. "Malo" or "MLF" for short, it's the process by which tart, tangy malic acid is converted into softer, creamier lactic acid (yup, like what's in cheese and milk). It's also what gives us "creamy," hence why "buttery" and "creamy" are frequent tasting-notes partners. And since barrel aging tends to encourage malo, you can expect "oaky" to tag along in those descriptions, too.

The point is that Chardonnay is not the only wine that can be described as "buttery"; any number of white wine grapes that have undergone malo can—but it *is* the most iconic because of how trendy it was to make creamy, buttery Chardonnay in the 1980s and '90s. It's decidedly less so these days, now that lighter, leaner, higher-acid expressions of Chardonnay (and wine in general, really) have gained in popularity. But if you're of the "more butter, more better" persuasion, you can definitely still find wines that fit the bill, usually from New World regions (i.e., North and South America, Australia, New Zealand, and South Africa).

"If you tend to like an oaky, buttery Chardonnay, I don't think this Grüner Veltliner will be for you—it's much lighter and leaner, with more acidity and distinctive vegetal notes."

BRIOCHE

When your wine gives out aromas of bread week on *The Great British Bake Off*: yeasty, sweet buttery, fresh-outta-the-oven golden toasty. Fittingly, this rich note of French bread is most often associated with France's most iconic fizz, Champagne. But it's not the French connection that links them, it's the yeast. Specifically, it's because when Champagne (and other Champagne-method sparklings, such as Cava and crémant) are made, the wines see extended contact with the lees, the spent yeast cells leftover from fermentation. Bubbs aside, you can also come across the aroma in still whites that have been stirred with, or aged on, the lees. Think Chardonnay, Sémillon, and some Muscadet labeled *sur lie* (literally, "on the lees").

"The Champagne we opened for New Year's Eve dinner had a delightful bouquet of grilled brioche, lemon curd, and toasted almond."

TOASTY

Your flavor clue that the wine—could be white, red, or even sparkling—has been aged in oak barrels that have been well charred/toasted. (More on this and other wine-aging vessels in "Keep Pouring" on page 100.) Confusingly, wine described this way smells and tastes more like dark caramel or butterscotch and borderline-burnt roasted nuts than actual toast. You can expect to find examples of this in Champagne and Champagne-method sparklings; Chardonnays (oak-aged, obviously, from places such as Burgundy, California, Australia, and New Zealand) and white Riojas; reds from Bordeaux and Bordeaux-style red blends, Syrahs, Zinfandels, and Tempranillo from Rioja.

"The white Burgundy I tried last night opened with these elegant, delicate toasty aromas of roasted hazelnut and brown butter."

The Difference a Vessel Can Make

For a winemaker, choosing which type of vessel to use for fermentation and aging is not dissimilar from a chef choosing which techniques to use when creating a dish. Winemakers have to consider what the desired outcomes are in terms of flavor and texture and what is best for the specific ingredient they're working with. Certain grapes and styles of wine are better suited to certain vessels, and only certain vessels can impart certain flavors and textures.

Here is a quick overview of different vessels, why they're used, and the impact they can have on a wine.

Wood Barrel

A wood barrel is kind of like those seven-in-one pans: a single vessel that provides a lot of different functions. For one thing, it's porous, so it allows for teeny-tiny-itty-bitty amounts of oxygen to interact with the wine (aka microoxygenation), which helps soften and round out a wine's texture by mellowing the feel of acidity and tannins. It can impart new aromas and flavors, which is why it is *not* usually the preferred choice for super aromatic varietals such as Gewürztraminer and Torrontès. Not to mention that it can add oomph to a wine's body by contributing to its tannic structure, as well as increase the ageability of the wine (aka its aging potential, aka how long you can keep it in bottle and still have it taste good when you open it), since tannins act like a preservative.

The specifics and degree of a wood barrel's impact depend on a few variables:

- **The type of wood used.** Oak is most common, but barrels can also be made from acacia and chestnut.

- **Where the wood is from.** French oak, for example, has a tighter grain and tends to have a delicate influence, typically giving a wine a smoother texture and imparting notes of cedar, tobacco, and spice. American oak is wider grained, known for having a more assertive presence and lending vanilla, coconut, and dill flavors.

- **The size.** The smaller the barrel, the more wine is in contact with the wood and therefore the stronger an impression it leaves on the wine's flavor and texture.

- **The toast.** "Toast" is the level of char on the wood inside the barrel. The more toast, the more charred/smoky/roasty flavors are imparted to the wine. (The toasting process takes place before any wine goes into the barrel. Winemakers buy barrels with specific toast levels based on their needs.)

- **The age.** "New oak" means that the barrel is brand spankin' new, never been used. The newer the wood, the bigger the impact.

Generally, after three years of holding wine, a barrel is rebranded as "neutral"—desirable for winemakers who want the micro-oxygenation effect but aren't looking for the barrel to impart flavor and tannin. Because the wood has been used to hold wine before, the strength of its impact and what it imparts to the wine lessens. You could think about it as being like the difference between an infusion made with fruit or spices that have never been used to do so before versus one made with fruit or spices that have been used to make several infusions. The flavor imparted by new oak will be more concentrated than that imparted by neutral oak.

Stainless-Steel Tank

Generally speaking, this is the vessel of choice for wines that are all about showcasing crisp freshness and the "true," no-makeup-on fruit flavors of the grape(s). Because they're airtight and temperature controlled and have a neutral flavor impact, they're ideal for highly aromatic grape varietals, lighter-bodied wines (especially whites but reds, too), and wines that are intended to be drunk young.

Amphora

A large, urn-shaped clay vessel that dates back to ancient times (like, 6000 BCE ancient) but has recently reentered the chat in a significant way thanks to its frequent use in the production of skin-contact white wines (aka orange wines) and some natural wines. Fun fact: In the republic of Georgia, considered the OGs of making orange wine, the vessels are called *qvevri* (*kweh*-vree).

Think of amphorae as being a little bit like a happy medium between wood barrels and stainless-steel tanks: porous like the former, allowing for micro-air exchange that gives the wine a rounder texture, and neutral like the latter, preserving the flavor and aroma of the grape varietal(s). Though they are most often used for orange wines, some examples of their being used to make rosés and reds exist. Aside from Georgia, northeastern Italy, Slovenia, and the United States are great places to look for wines fermented and/or aged in amphorae.

Concrete Egg

Like an amphora, this is a kind of "best of both worlds" vessel—it literally looks like a large concrete egg with legs—that allows for some oxygen exchange but is flavor neutral. The thing people seem to talk a lot about with concrete eggs is the "vortex effect" that the shape creates. It helps keep the lees in suspension throughout the wine instead of falling to the bottom of the barrel or tank, which proponents believe helps enhance a wine's flavor and texture.

Oaky vs. Nonoaky Wine

For this "A Tale of Two Chardonnays" exercise, you're going to need one that's been fermented and aged in stainless steel and one that's been aged in new oak. How do the two differ in terms of aroma? The stainless steel one should give you more straightforward fruit flavors, while the oak one should deliver more nonfruit, savory flavors, such as butter, roasted nuts, and baking spices. And what about what's going on with the texture, the way it feels in your mouth? See how the one that's aged in oak feels richer and rounder on your palate versus the stainless-steel expression, which is leaner with brighter acidity?

Like, Totally Psychedelic

Talking About Acidity

There is no overstating the important role that acidity plays in wine. Its ability to brighten and refresh, provide contrast, and cut through richness is what makes wine such a great beverage to pair with food. It's also one of the elements that acts as a natural preservative and helps keep a wine in good condition as it ages. And, frankly, without it, a wine cannot be balanced; it's a key structural element that keeps other components such as sweetness, alcohol, and tannin in check.

Wine nerds basically pray at the altar of it and crave it in almost absurdly high doses. Of course, as with anything when it comes to wine and wine tasting, your personal threshold for appreciating high acidity levels is subjective. But since wine peeps tend to be shameless acid junkies, keep in mind that the following creative ways to say "This wine has a f*ck-ton of acidity" are generally used in a positive sense. Happy acid tripping!

CRISP

Brisk and refreshing, like a cool fall breeze. Or that first crunchy-sour bite into a perfectly ripe, picked-from-the-orchard apple. When the acidity is high but also still approachable.

"This crisp Vermentino is perfect patio-lunch-date wine. So refreshing; it tastes like salty citrus laced with fresh herbs."

Acidity with a strong mineral edge. Sharp and cool like the blade of a sword, the tart, sour flavors cut right across your palate.

STEELY

"Talk about some steely acidity on that Mosel Riesling! The lemony green apple tartness is slicing right across my palate."

BRIGHT

When the intensity of the acidity makes it feel as though the fruit flavors are glowing in your mouth. It gives the wine a sense of freshness and vibrancy that makes it feel high toned. It's a popular tasting note for youthful wines that are lighter bodied with higher acidity levels and a leaner fruit profile. For whites, think Sauvignon Blanc, Muscadet, Albariño, Vermentino, Pinot Grigio, and Grüner Veltliner; for reds, cool-climate Pinot Noir, Gamay, Barbera, Frappato, Zweigelt, and Mencía are great places to start. It can be used in association with specific fruit notes or to describe the overall personality of a wine.

"Loving the superbright cherry and strawberry notes on this Zweigelt!"

When the energy of the acidity makes it feel as though it's the kind of wine that springs out of bed at 6:00 a.m. without the help of seven alarms set to go off every five minutes. Bright-eyed and bushy-tailed. It's often assigned to younger, very fresh-tasting wines (any of those mentioned under "Bright" could apply here, too) but could also describe an older wine that feels particularly youthful.

LIVELY

"Wow, I didn't expect a fifteen-year-old Rioja to feel this lively, but the acidity is still driving!"

ZIPPY

When that acidity is buzzin' around your mouth, zipping up and down, side to side with unbridled glee.

"Have you tried that Assyrtiko yet? All that zippy citrus acidity is totally mouthwatering."

When the intensity of the acidity makes the wine feel as though it's had one too many cups of coffee. It's a palpable vibrancy that leaves your tongue tingling.

NERVY

"The acidity of that Picpoul is so vibrant and nervy, it woke my palate right up."

SNAPPY   This is the word to use when a wine's sour, tangy acidity hits your tongue like the sharp crack of a whip.

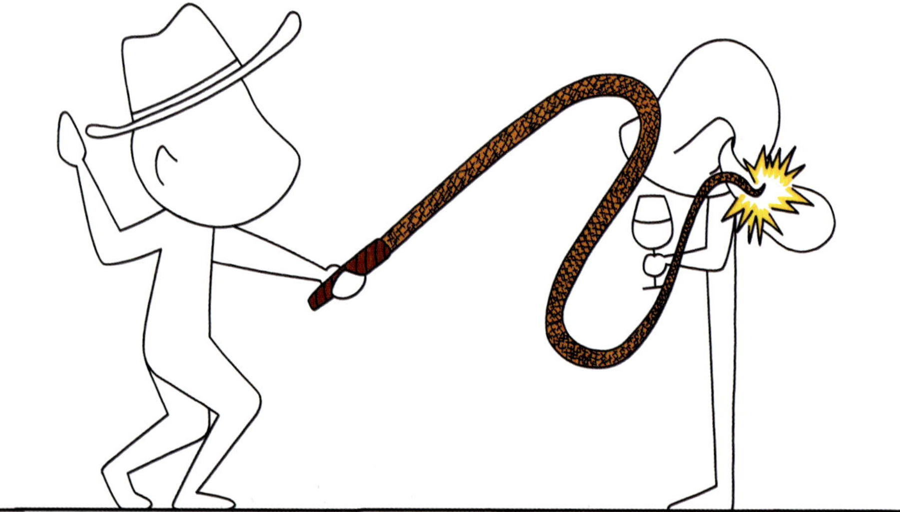

"The notes of tart red currant and underripe strawberry lend a snappy acidity to this rosé."

Mike Tyson's in your mouth, uppercutting and throwing jabs with lemon-lime gloves on.

PUNCHY

"I see why you like drinking Vinho Verde with ceviche—the punchy acidity in the wine complements the citrus in the dish."

RACY

The acidity is zooming down your palate at record speed as though it's on an F1 track—fast, flashy, full of energy. You can feel where it leaves tire marks.

"You can always count on a Sauvignon Blanc from Sancerre to deliver on racy acidity. It felt like a trio of lemon, grapefruit, and green apple whizzing down my palate in a Ferrari at breakneck speed."

When the acidity is so intense, pure, and focused
that it cuts across your palate like a frickin'
laser beam. It's got vibrancy and razor's-edge
precision, like the *schrvmmmm-kwishhh* of Luke
Skywalker's lightsaber coming to life.

LASER-LIKE

*"The briny, lemony, laser-like acidity of this Muscadet is going to be such
a good match for everything in our shellfish tower. I'm pumped."*

ELECTRIC

I'm not advocating that you try this at home, but what you might imagine it would feel like to stick your tongue into an electrical socket. Or if it was stung by a jellyfish. Leaves you buzzin'.

"The acidity in this young Chenin Blanc is absolutely electric—fistfuls of crunchy quince, green apple, and sharp lemon curd."

No, but seriously, is the acidity *trying* to shred
your tongue to pieces? Maybe? Probably?
Who cares; you like it.

"As expected, the acidity of this Mosel Riesling is ripping, just so sharp and
cutting across the palate. It gives the wine a real liveliness."

SCREAMING When the acidity is about as subtle as the vocalist of a metalcore band. It's high-pitched mic-to-the-mouth wailing that pierces your soul and leaves you vibrating—and craving more.

"*If you like a bone-dry expression of Riesling, you have to try this one from Australia—the acidity is screaming.*"

FLABBY

When a wine feels like you might if you ditched your gym routine: lacking firmness and structure. It's most often something you notice when the wine doesn't have enough acidity. The wine is unbalanced, just jiggle-wiggling limply on your palate without anything to hold it together.

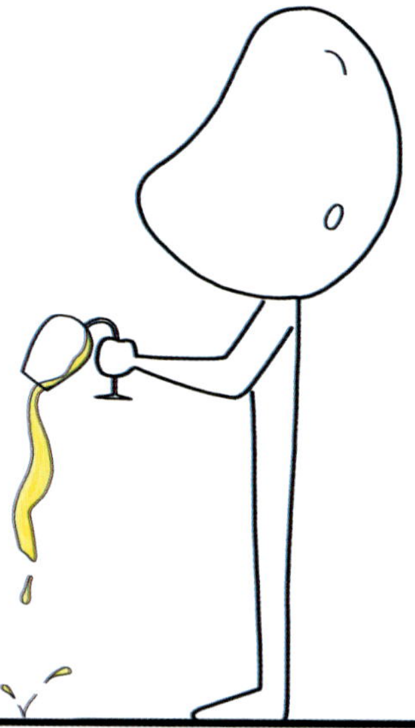

"This white feels a bit flabby. I wish there was a little more acidity for brightness and lift."

Just blah. Where is the energy? The brightness?
The personality? The structure? Again, this
is often the result of a wine's lacking acidity.
Unrelated to acidity, the term is also used to
describe a sparkling wine that's lost its sparkle.

"I know Viognier is a naturally low-acid varietal, but this one feels
surprisingly flat on the palate. The flavors of overripe stone fruit are so
overtly generous, I wish there was a touch more zing of acidity to lift it
up and balance the richness."

Feelin' It

Talking About Texture and Mouthfeel

A lot of time and effort are put into trying to identify *what* wine tastes like. But flavor isn't the only thing that should be on your mind when you're sipping. You should also be considering *how* wine tastes. What does wine feel like when it hits your tongue and travels around the inside of your mouth? There are a lot of possible ways to describe just that.

Full disclosure, friends: We've got a *lot* to cover in this chapter, so buckle up, it's a long one. We'll start with the category of wine that has the most obvious tactile experience, which is sparkling. We'll cover the words you need to know to talk bubbly, and I'll give you a cheat sheet to the various styles from around the world.

But there's plenty of texture in still wines to talk about—words related to body and weight, and tannin, of course. You're familiar with tannin and its many aliases, right? If not, you definitely will be after this section.

Before we jump in, let me just preface this chapter by saying that wine texture can be a tough nut to crack. It's not like food texture, where the difference between how gelato feels on your tongue (smooth) versus a mouthful of chips (crunchy) is pretty obvious. With still wine especially, there are a lot of nuances and subtle variations between words for texture that may seem synonymous. It's not necessarily easy to differentiate between light and lean versus full and round. Or know if, when tasting a high-tannin red, you should refer to it as "grippy" instead of "stiff." It takes practice.

And like all wine tasting, it's personal! So go ahead and familiarize yourself with the lingo, but don't get too bogged down by the nitty-gritty. Try a lot of different styles of wine side by side, and go with the words in the following pages that speak to you.

No, not like the kind you use when you make your Swiftie friendship bracelets. In winespeak, it's what you call the string of bubbles that rises up the side of your glass of sparkling wine. Typically, if the bead is persistent and long-lasting, it means that the wine is well made and of good quality. The term can also be used when trying to describe the size and texture of a sparkling wine's bubbles, i.e., a "fine" bead versus a "coarse" bead. A "fine" bead = smaller, more precise bubbles, generally considered a sign of higher quality. A "coarse" bead = larger, fatter bubbles.

BEAD

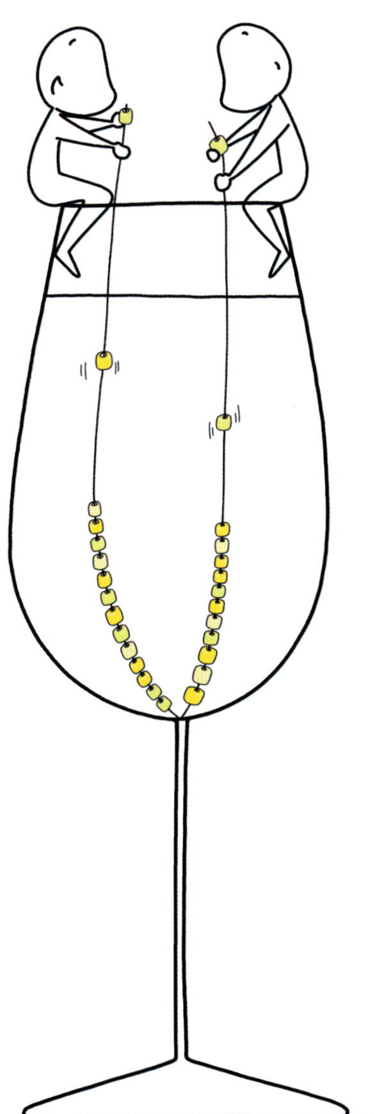

"Check out the bead on this Champagne: superfine and persistent."

FIZZ

Casual, slangy, trying-to-sound-cool sub for "sparkling wine." The same person who calls wine "juice"* probably calls sparkling wine "fizz."

---

*For those who are unfamiliar with the term, "juice" is a somewhat trendy euphemism for wine (as in *"Dude, I'm geeking out. This wine bar is slingin' some sick juice!"*). For a moment in time it gave off insider "I know and give a shit about wine but, like, in a cool and nonchalant kind of way." But these days it seems to have drifted into the realm of coming off a bit . . . [checks over shoulders to see if anyone listening might get pissed] . . . douchey. (Sorry.)

"Want to start with a couple glasses of fizz and then move on to a bottle with dinner?"

PEARL

Like "bead" but when the string of bubbs has accumulated on the surface of the wine in the glass, along the perimeter, resembling, you guessed it, a pearl necklace. You can thank the French for this one—they are responsible for Champagne, after all, so it tracks—as the term comes from *pérlage*, which means "string of pearls."

"The pearl of this Champagne is so soft and delicate; it has a real walking-on-air kind of elegance."

When the bubbles are so small and well defined
that they feel sharp on your tongue, like a
thousand delightful tiny pinpricks.

PRICKLY

*"The sharp, prickly texture of this sparkling gives it such a vibrant and
lively personality."*

SPRITZY

How you might describe a wine with a very light, very soft, barely there kind of effervescence. Whites and rosés from Txakolina in Spain's Basque region are the epitome of this. It's not exactly bubbly, it's spritzy.

"Txakolina is my go-to patio wine—delightfully spritzy with punchy acidity, it's all I want on a hot summer afternoon."

Like the head on a pint of beer, it's the bubble bath–like foam that accumulates on the surface of a glass of sparkling wine. (Aka what spills over the top of the glass when you pour too fast. Don't worry, we've all done it.) Some also use the term to describe a sparkling wine with creamier, fatter bubbles.

MOUSSE

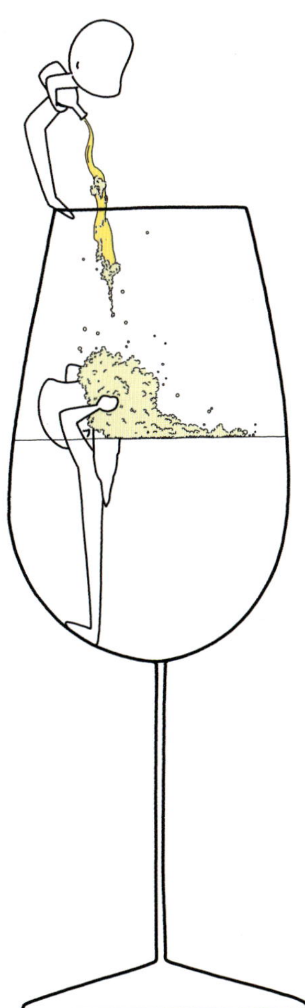

"The mousse on this Crémant almost has a frothy kind of quality; it adds a nice fullness to the palate."

Sparkling Wine, a Cheat Sheet

All wines technically go through a sparkling phase. Remember, when unfermented grape juice and yeast get together, they make alcohol and CO_2. If you're making a still wine, those bubbles just get the "Let it go! Let it go!" treatment, released into the ether, so to speak. If you're making a sparkling wine, you've got to trap those bubbles, either during the initial, primary fermentation process or, more commonly, during an induced secondary fermentation (more on that in a moment). How a bottle of bubbs gets its bubbs, where it's made, and what grapes it's made from are the main factors in differentiating one type of sparkling wine from another. Here's a little primer to help you navigate the fine world of fizz.

Champagne

Where: Must be produced in Champagne, France, from grapes grown in the Champagne region.

Grape(s): Made with one or a combination of three varietals: Chardonnay, Pinot Noir, Pinot Meunier.[*]

How it's made: You make a still wine (primary fermentation), then bottle it with a little added sugar and yeast. That duo goes to work, causing another fermentation (secondary fermentation) to take place in the bottle. This process introduces bubbles to the party and they remain trapped. If you're going to remember one thing, *remember this secondary fermentation in the bottle thing*; it's what makes the Champagne method, aka *méthode traditionnelle*, the Champagne method.

After the wine has been aged for a certain length of time (depending on variables

[*] Actually, seven grapes are *legally* allowed to be used, but those are the main three; the other four are *much* less frequently encountered.

such as the producer's house style, regional regulations, and winemaking goals), the lees are removed from the bottle to clarify the wine. Then comes the addition of a little *dosage*, a sugar-wine solution that determines the dryness/sweetness level of the final wine, before it's resealed with a cork and cage (the metal cap with wires that keeps the cork in place).

Sweetness levels: *Brut nature* (as dry as they come) → *extra brut* (still super dry) → *brut* (dry) → extra dry (confusingly, less dry and slightly sweeter than *brut*) → *demi-sec* (semisweet/off dry) → *doux* (sweet).

WORDS TO KNOW

- ***Blanc de Blancs:*** Literally "white from whites," it means that the Champagne is made from 100 percent Chardonnay.

- ***Blanc de Noirs:*** Literally "white from reds," it means that the Champagne is made from the red grapes Pinot Noir and/or Pinot Meunier but is white/clear because it was pressed off the skins.

- ***Nonvintage (NV):*** Most Champagnes are blends of wines made in different years, or vintages. Because there can be so much variation in the wines from year to year, making NV blends allows Champagne houses to consistently maintain their signature house style.

- ***Vintage:*** When the wine used to make the Champagne comes from a single vintage. This happens only in years deemed to be exceptional, so they're considered more special and, *of course*, are going to be more expensive.

- ***Special/prestige/tête de cuvée:*** A Champagne house's top bottling, such as Dom Pérignon for Moët & Chandon, Cuvée Sir Winston Churchill for Pol Roger, and Cristal for Louis Roederer.

- ***Grower Champagne:*** Not something you'll likely see on a label, but you might hear it talked about in a restaurant or wine shop, as it's very trendy among wine pros. It just means that the grapes used to make the wine are owned and grown by the producer, as opposed to being purchased. This may not sound like that big a deal, but it's the exception and not the norm in the region. It's an indication that it's a smaller, more hands-on kind of Champagne producer—more family-owned restaurant versus big franchise vibes.

Sparkling Wines Made like Champagne but Outside Champagne

Around the world, many regions outside Champagne make excellent traditional-method sparkling wines. They are a great value because they don't command the same high prices that Champagne naturally does; Champagne has done an A+ job at marketing itself and cementing the region's association with luxury. Plus, they offer the opportunity to experience a wider range of varietals and *terroirs*.

TYPES OF WINE

- *Crémant:* From other parts of France, made with the grapes of the region. For example, Chenin Blanc for Crémant de la Loire; Riesling, Pinot Gris, and Pinot Blanc for Crémant d'Alsace; Savagnin, Poulsard, and Trousseau for Crémant du Jura.

- *Franciacorta:* From Lombardy, Italy, made mostly from Pinot Noir and Chardonnay plus sometimes a little Pinot Blanc.

- *Cava:* From Penedès in northeastern Spain, using Xarello, Macabeo, and Parellada for white and Garnacha and Monastrell for rosé.

- *Winzersekt:* From Germany, usually made with Riesling.

- *Sekt Reserve and Grosse Reserve:* From Austria; most commonly made with Grüner Veltliner and Welschriesling.

- *English sparkling wine:* Bet you can guess where this is from. Usually made with Chardonnay and Pinot Noir.

- *Cap Classique:* From South Africa; can be made with any varietal.

- *American sparkling wine:* Actually, there is no designated name for American wines made in this style, but you can look for something such as "traditional method" or a dryness level designation such as *brut* on the label. Plus it'll have a cork-and-cage closure. Most come from California and are made with the three classic Champagne grapes.

Sparkling Wines Not Made like Champagne

These bottles get their bubbly using different techniques that produce varying flavors, characteristics, and textures.

CHARMAT METHOD. Also known as the "tank method" or "Prosecco method" since it is famous for its use in producing that popular Italian sparkling wine. Much easier to scale than the traditional method, the big difference with this technique is that the second fermentation occurs in a large, pressurized steel tank instead of individual bottles. The result is a sparkling wine with a softer fizz and a lighter, fruitier profile. Popular examples of this method include:

- **Prosecco:** From the Veneto and Friuli regions of northeastern Italy, made using the Glera grape.

- **Lambrusco:** From Italy's Emilia-Romagna region, made using the Lambrusco grape. Can be red or rosé and range from very dry to sweet.

- **Moscato d'Asti and Asti Spumante:** From Italy's Piedmont region, made in a sweet style from the Muscat grape.

- **Sekt:** From Germany and Austria, where Riesling and Grüner star, respectively.

PÉTILLANT NATUREL METHOD. Also known as *méthode ancestrale* or, as the cool kids call it, *pét-nat*. It's distinguished by the fact that it undergoes only a primary fermentation. Instead of making a still wine and then having it undergo a secondary fermentation, as in the Champagne method, *pét-nats* are bottled during the initial fermentation process, which traps the CO_2 bubbles.

While this low-to-no-intervention, no-regulations method is actually the oldest way of making sparkling wine, it has seen a huge resurgence in recent years thanks to its popularity in the natural wine scene. Expect the wine to be cloudy (since the lees aren't removed), feature a bottle cap closure, and have a softer, frothier fizz than Champagne. Examples come in a range of varietals from all over the wine-growing world, but France and the United States in particular make a lot of it.

That covers the texture and mouthfeel specifics of sparkling wine. Now on to the rest of the words you need to know to talk texture.

Sparkling Wine Off

Think all sparkling wines taste the same? Play a round of this, and come back to me. For this game we're pulling examples of three different wines that get their sparkle from three different methods. You're going to need a Champagne-method sparkling (Champagne or crémant, if you want to keep it more wallet friendly); a charmat-method sparkling (Prosecco); and a *pét-nat* sparkling. What do you notice about how they look? Appearance-wise, the Champagne and the Prosecco probably look similar, but see how the *pét-nat* is cloudy and has sediment floating around in it? What about the bubbles—how do they differ? Which one has the sharpest, most persistent bubbles, and which ones dissipate more quickly? Does one taste prickly and another more frothy-foamy? What about the flavors? Notice how the Champagne has more yeasty-toasty-nutty notes, whereas the Prosecco has more clean fruit flavors? And how about that *pét-nat*? A little funk there?

Think of wine as being like a house: It has building blocks, elements that give it a framework and a shape in your mouth, things such as the sugar and alcohol levels, but particularly acidity and tannin. The last are like the mortar holding the bricks together.

When a wine has high levels of acidity and tannin, that's when you'd describe it as being very "structured." On the flip side of the coin, when it seems as though a wine doesn't have much structure, that's when you could characterize it as feeling soft or flabby (as though it's lacking acidity; see page 120).

When all the building blocks feel evenly matched, you'd describe the wine as having a "well-balanced" structure. It's passing the home inspection; it's sound. What's more, it's better equipped to stand the test of time. A good structure is essential to a wine's aging potential.

But remember that a wine's structure is going to be impacted by things such as the grape(s) it's made from and where it's grown. A Pinot Noir from Willamette Valley is never going to have the same structure as a Tempranillo from Rioja. It's better to compare the Pinot Noir to another expression of the varietal from a different region, such as Burgundy or Sonoma; or the Tempranillo to another medium-bodied,

STRUCTURE/
STRUCTURED

higher-tannin red, such as a Sangiovese. The point is, you can't compare apples to oranges. Still, you can find examples of each that, in their own right, are well structured and have the ability to age. You just have to do a little homework (fun homework! drinking wine homework!) to get an understanding of what to expect from a given grape.

"The structure of this Chianti is great: tons of lively red fruit acidity matched with firm tannins."

This is another way of saying "This wine has a good, solid structure." Sometimes a specific characteristic—usually minerality, when describing a white—is the source of the backbone.

"I love the way the mineral backbone supports the ripe tropical fruit notes."

"The Cabernet Sauvignon in this Bordeaux blend gives the wine such a strong backbone: stiff tannins with lots of plush fruit and lively acidity to match."

FRAMED BY Use this phrase when you don't just want to say simply that a wine has a "nice structure" but are looking to paint a more complete and descriptive picture, calling out the specific structural components holding it together. It's probably a little over the top to use in a casual "Let's talk about this wine" conversation—you're not going to go out to a restaurant and ask for a wine that's "nicely framed by fine-grained tannins and zippy acidity." That would be a bit much. But it is used by professionals writing tasting notes for wine publications, for example.

"A dazzling display of ripe tropical fruit, wild rose, and a hint of ginger spice, framed by a wet stone minerality and electric acidity."

Think about what biting into a just-barely-ripe cranberry or green apple feels like: sharp and snappy. It's juicy but also slightly rigid, as though there's a delicate friction in the way it interacts with your gums and tastebuds. That's what drinking a "crunchy" wine feels like. Some people associate this term with a high acidity level, others with prominent tannins, sometimes both. It's not a reflection of a wine's being good or bad, although generally it's perceived as being more enjoyable than not; it's just a description of a sensory experience. Expect to find this in wines (red or white) that are younger, lighter bodied, not too high in alcohol, and not aged in new oak.

CRUNCHY

"I'm obsessed with how crunchy some of these Loire Valley reds are. So fresh and lean, and completely quaffable."

CHISELED   Think well defined, precise, laser cut—everything my muscles could be if I exercised and stopped drinking so much wine. The term is most often used to describe lighter-to-medium-bodied white wines with bright, cutting acidity and strong mineral notes, for example, Chablis, Muscadet, Albariño, Assyrtiko, or Austrian Riesling.

"That Chablis feels like it was literally cut from limestone—the combo of steely acidity and minerality gives it such a chiseled quality on the palate."

ANGULAR

Understandably, this term could easily be confused with "chiseled." It's made all the more confusing by the fact that generally the word has a negative connotation, whereas "chiseled" leans positive. It's when the sharp quality of the wine's texture, caused by overly intense acidity and/or tannins, hits your palate in a way that doesn't feel balanced with the rest of the wine's components. It kind of sticks out like an awkward, pointy sore thumb. It's distracting and overpowering.

"Something's not working here; it feels very angular. The acidity is coming on suuuuuper strong. I wish there was a little more roundness to the fruit to balance it out."

FAT

When a wine feels the way we all do after Thanksgiving dinner: full bodied and high in alcohol content. Wines that fit this description usually also have lower acidity and softer tannins, coupled with rich fruit flavors. There's a heaviness to the sip, as though a weighted blanket was just pulled over your palate. It's not necessarily a dig but not exactly a compliment, either.

"This Marsanne-Roussanne blend definitely drinks a bit fat, bigger than the Chenin for sure, but that little bit of acidity at the end helps lift it up."

Like "fat," except you're making it clear that you're using it as a diss.

"Whoa, that Priorat is hea-vy. Like, superrich. What is the ABV at? Sixteen percent?"

Talking About Body

Talking about a wine's body is code for its "weight." Don't worry; in the world of wine, weight isn't a taboo, don't-go-there topic. It's standard practice, a reference point for categorizing and differentiating among various grapes and wines in an easy-to-digest, broad-strokes kind of way: light, medium, full.

What you're trying to assess is: How do the viscosity and density of the wine feel as it glides across your palate? Is the wine light and delicate, like a thin top sheet? Or is it dense and coating, like a heavy wool blanket? Does it feel like drinking skim milk or slurping on an extra-thick milkshake? Or somewhere in between?

A wine's weight is the result of a combination of various influences:

- *Booze level.* Higher-alcohol wines (14+ percent ABV) taste heavier, lower-alcohol wines (<12 percent) taste lighter.

- *Acidity level.* A wine will taste lighter if the acidity level is screaming, ripping, laser-like, electric . . .

- *Sugar level.* A wine with higher residual sugar, such as a dessert wine, will taste fuller bodied, kind of like how a diet soda tastes lighter than a regular one.

- *Tannin level.* Because tannin contributes to a wine's structure, red wines with higher tannin levels will feel heavier and more substantial in the mouth.

- *Climate.* Grapes grown in warmer climates tend to produce wines that are fuller bodied because they're riper and have a lower acidity.[*]

- *Winemaking choices.* Things such as aging a wine in oak barrels or on its lees can contribute to its tasting fuller bodied.

- *Grape variety.* Sometimes it's a matter of genetics! Some varietals naturally produce lighter-bodied wines, while others produce fuller-bodied wines.

---

[*] That's not a hard-and-fast rule, of course, because those basically don't exist in wine.

Here's a general idea of where various grape varieties land on the body scale. (I say "general" because, of course, various factors—environmental, how it's made, the winemaker's stylistic choices, etc.—will have an influence on the final wine produced.)

WHITE: LIGHT TO FULL	RED: LIGHT TO FULL
Melon de Bourgogne	Gamay
Aligoté	Cinsault
Assyrtiko	Pinot Noir
Albariño	Frappato
Grüner Veltliner	Barbera
Furmint	Zweigelt
Pinot Blanc	Nerello Mascalese
Verdejo	Blaufränkisch
Verdicchio	Dolcetto
Sylvaner	Montepulciano
Godello	Carménère
Muscat	Cabernet Franc
Pinot Grigio/Pinot Gris	Sangiovese
Vermentino	Tempranillo
Garganega	Grenache
Riesling	Nebbiolo
Sauvignon Blanc	Merlot
Chenin Blanc	Nero d'Avola
Arneis	Zinfandel
Fiano	Malbec
Torrontés	Mourvèdre
Ribolla Gialla	Xinomavro
Gewürztraminer	Syrah
Chardonnay	Cabernet Sauvignon
Marsanne	Touriga Nacional
Roussanne	Pinotage
Sémillon	Aglianico
Viognier	Petite Sirah
	Tannat

LEAN

When you take a sip and the wine's texture feels sharp, tight, and kind of austere, like sleeping on an extra-firm mattress. Look for fruit flavor that is more on the tart, underripe side and a racy acidity that zips down your palate straight as a razor's edge. Whether or not you're into this style of wine is a matter of personal preference.

"The Grüner Veltliner was a great choice with this dish. Super lean with racy acidity; it felt like it cut right down the middle of my palate."

Used to describe fuller-bodied reds that have a dark, opaque hue, concentrated fruit flavor, and a rich, palate-coating texture. This term is easy to remember and point out because the pigment of the wine will literally stain the glass. Think Zinfandel, Petite Sirah, and Cabernet Sauvignon from California, Argentinian Malbec, Aglianico from southern Italy, and Australian Shiraz.

"I forgot how inky Petite Sirah is—such a rich, opaque purple in the glass, and that concentrated note of blackberry jam really coats the palate."

RICH

Like taking a big bite of double-fudge flourless chocolate cake: dense, mouth coating, and full flavored. It's a frequent tasting notes partner with "concentrated" and "ripe"; use it to describe wines (usually red) that are big on fruit and moderate on acidity.

"This Châteauneuf-du-Pape is rich! Offering ripe flavors of dark forest berries, dried herbs, and wild game."

Imagine biting into a just slightly overripe peach, plum, or slice of mango: smooth, juicy, pulpy, plump. It's like that sensation. This is a frequent tasting notes partner with "concentrated"; expect to find it in wines (red and white) that are more fruit forward, fuller bodied, and higher in alcohol.

FLESHY

"Bursting with ripe tropical and stone fruit notes, super fleshy on the palate."

OILY

When the texture of the wine has a slightly viscous, almost slippery quality. Think of the way olive oil feels on your tongue compared to water. It's associated mostly with white wines, specifically ones that are fuller bodied with lower acidity. Classic examples of wines with this texture include Viognier, Gewürztraminer, Sémillon, Garganega (aka Soave), and Pinot Gris (specifically from Alsace or Oregon).

"You can really feel the Sémillon in this white Bordeaux, huh? That oily, palate-coating texture is such a dead giveaway for me."

CREAMY

A rare wine descriptor that actually means what it sounds like: The wine feels rich, round, and smooth, as though it has some weight to it, and coats your palate. Think gelato vs. granita. The product of malolactic fermentation, expect to notice it most in white wines that have been aged in oak—grapes such as Chardonnay, Sémillon, Marsanne, Roussanne, and Viognier are good candidates. "Creamy" can also pop up in descriptions of Champagnes and Champagne-method sparklings, but in those cases, it tends to reference flavor (as in, it tastes like cream, like what you might put in your coffee) rather than texture. You can often find it partnered with "brioche" in the pastry case flavor profile collection.

"This Santa Barbara Chardonnay has a pleasant creaminess to it, full and rich on the palate, with layers of lemon curd, baked apple, and vanilla."

THIN

When you come to a glass hoping for bisque but the wine gives you watered-down broth. It means you think that not only the body and texture but also overall depth of flavor are lackluster and do not live up to your expectations of the wine. Less is not more. This is not to be confused with "lean," which is generally used as a positive way of describing a light-bodied wine with sharpness and precision. (I know, I know, these are the fine discrepancies that can set the eye rolls in motion and turn people off of wine.)

"That's disappointing—it's pretty on the nose, but the texture on the midpalate is super thin; it just disappears."

Generally used in reference to easy-drinking, well-balanced red wines with soft or very well integrated tannins that aren't too in your face. Typically, smooth red wines will also be medium to full bodied, with moderate acidity, and relatively fruit forward. Think California or Washington State Merlot, Argentinian Malbec, and Grenache-based wines from France's southern Rhône Valley.

SMOOTH*

---

* Warning: This term is frequently bemoaned by industry pros because it has become so overused. It's like a song that is played over and over again to the point where it starts to lose its meaning. Not only that, it's the perception (I'd say *misperception*) that smoothness equals high quality. Or smoothness equals good, better. If you want to avoid causing eye rolls, try not to *only* say "smooth" when asked what quality you like or are looking for in a wine. By the end of this book you'll have so many more words up your sleeve, it (hopefully) shouldn't be difficult.

"*This Barbera has a smooth, silky texture with super-fine-grain tannins. It glides across the palate.*"

ROUND

A descriptor as ubiquitous as it is subjective. Some people use it as they would "smooth," when a wine is fuller with soft edges (that is, it has no stiff tannins or ripping acidity), making for an easy drinking experience. Others might use it to convey that they feel that the wine is balanced, that its major components are in proportion. Because of its gray area-ness, it's probably best not to use this as a stand-alone descriptor; include it as part of a larger tasting note to give context to how you're using it.

"I know Merlot isn't everyone's favorite, but I gotta say, this one's got a round, generous fruit quality that is really working for me right now. So easy to drink."

When it feels as though the wine is waltzing across your palate with the greatest of ease from the tip of your tongue to the back of your throat, effortlessly gliding with elegance and grace. Like "smooth" but not restricted to red wines and, let's be honest, a heck of a lot cooler sounding.

DANCES ACROSS THE PALATE

"I love the way that this Oregon Pinot Gris dances across the palate—feels like orchard fruit, citrus, and minerals are doing a very elegant Dancing with the Stars routine on my tongue."

SILKY

When you're tasting a red and it feels like putting on a slinky little black dress. "Smooth" with an element of luxury.

"The texture of this Merlot is so seductively silky; the tannins are really well integrated, so it just glides."

Like "silky" but with a hint more depth, weight, and richness of texture.

VELVETY

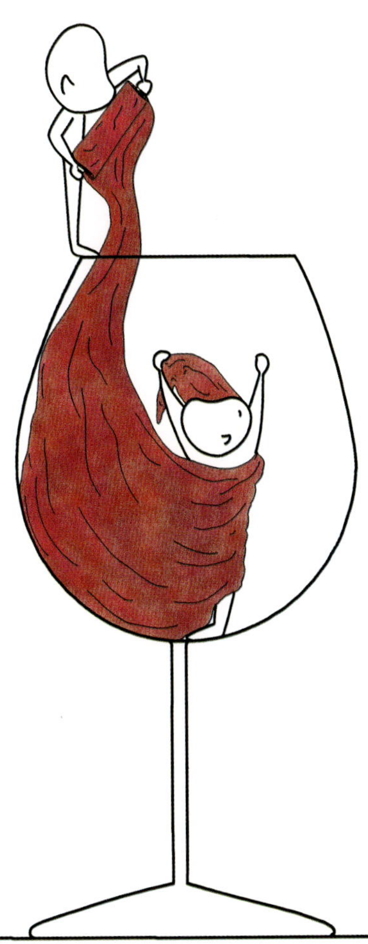

"Obsessed with the velvety texture of this Super Tuscan. It lends such a luxurious mouthfeel and gives it a real 'this tastes expensive' vibe."

Getting to Know Tannin, Dating Game Style

The final words in this (very long!) chapter on texture and mouthfeel all relate to tannin, the thing that causes that mouth-drying, stick-to-your-tongue-and-gums sensation when you drink red wine. To help you two get better acquainted, we're setting you up on a little "date" to cover all the need-to-know basics about this key wine component. (It's goofy, I know. I promise I wasn't drunk when I wrote it. Just trying to make learning about wine fun.)

Where are you from? Two places! I'm a polyphenol and antioxidant that occurs naturally in plants; so in grapes, I come from the skin, seeds, and stems. But when you notice me in wine, it can also be because of its being matured in wood barrels (especially newer wood barrels). So if you come across a wine that's been aged in new oak, you can expect to see me.

What are your favorite hangouts—i.e., where are you most likely to be found? Definitely always in reds, but some varietals are inherently more tannic than others:

- ***Low-tannin grapes:*** Gamay, Pinot Noir, Barbera, Cinsault, Frappato, Trousseau, Grenache

- ***High-tannin grapes:*** Cabernet Sauvignon, Syrah, Pinotage, Mourvèdre, Xinomavro, Aglianico, Nebbiolo

You can also find me in some rosés, especially darker-hued ones, and orange wines. The more concentrated color is an indication that the juice spent more time macerating with the grape skins.

Where are you least likely to be found? In white and sparkling wines (unless it's a sparkling red, such as Lambrusco).

Describe your personality in one word. Astringent. When you drink wine and feel that dry, bitter, cottonmouthy sensation on your palate and gums, it's because of me!

What do you bring to the relationship? Texture, structure, ageability, depth of color, and body.

Favorite food: Protein! The richer and fattier, the better. There's nothing I love more than a thick-cut, well-marbled steak served with a creamy sauce.

Dislikes: Anything spicy, oily fish, and super salty dishes. I also hate being cold; it makes me come across as extra harsh and bitter.

Nicknames: Depends on the circumstances. If I'm being chill: "velvety," "smooth," and "fine-grained"; if I'm being intense: "grippy," "stiff," "firm."

Best way to soften you up: Give me fresh air and time. Or a nice meal!

- *Air.* If my presence in a wine you've just opened feels too strong, try pouring it into a decanter; it won't lower the level of tannin in the wine, but it will mellow how it feels on the palate.

- *Time.* Tannin is a natural preservative, and while it helps wine age, it does break down over time. That's why wines made from more tannic grapes are usually best enjoyed in their more "mature" years—older vintages—after having had some time to age in bottle.

- *Food.* Sometimes when a wine has really strong tannins, it can feel overwhelming on your palate. But when you drink it alongside dishes containing protein and fat, they give the tannins something to cling onto besides your tongue and gums, creating a smoother, more balanced experience.

FINE GRAINED

When the texture of the tannins in the wine reminds you of walking on a beach where the sand feels like powder: soft, delicate, and light. You notice that the wine has tannin, but it doesn't stick out; it's well integrated into the wine. Basically, if you were to rate tannin level on a scale, "fine grained" would be at the lowest end and "grippy" or "firm" on the highest end.

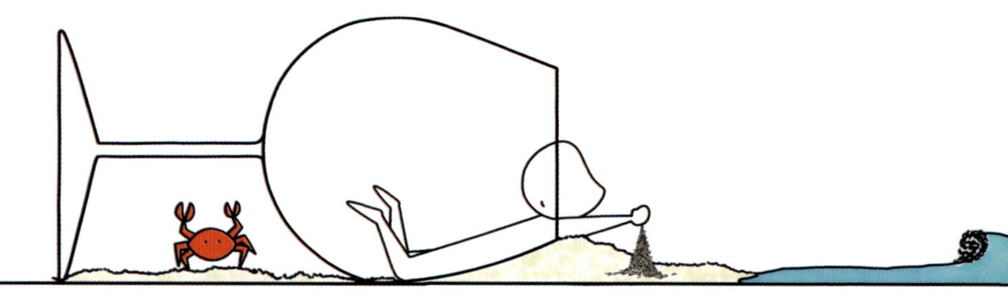

"This Pomerol is structured, but the tannins are so fine grained, it drinks really elegantly."

In the same wheelhouse as "fine grained," when the tannins have a kind of soft, dustlike texture and more of a noticeable presence on your palate. Unlike when someone uses the word to describe the cleanliness of your house (them be fightin' words), in regard to wine, "dusty" is not a bad or a good thing, just a thing. The same pretty much goes for other words used to describe the way tannins feel; they're just used as a qualitative assessment of the tannins' texture.

DUSTY

"*The dusty tannins on this Chianti Classico give it a rustic feel that lingers on the palate.*"

LEATHERY

"Leathery" is a common flavor cue in wines, but it can also be used to describe a wine that has a higher tannin level. Use it when you notice that the tannins are robust, with a slightly rough and unpolished quality; what it might feel like to lick the unfinished back side of a leather belt. (Not that I've ever done that in the name of research . . . nope, definitely not.)

"The tannins on this older vintage Barolo have a leathery quality that plays really nicely with the bouquet of earth, dried rose, and subtle spice."

When you taste a wine and it feels as though the tannins are giving your palate a solid, delivered-with-gusto handshake, the kind of tight hold you continue to feel long past the interaction. Use this term to describe a wine with a level of tannin that feels high in an unyielding kind of way. That's not necessarily a bad thing, but it can be a little intense and overwhelming.

It's often used to describe young red wines made from high-tannin grapes. Enjoying a "firm" wine with food could help balance out the overall experience, as could decanting it. But if you feel that neither of those things is softening the firmness, you might say that you think the wine needs some more time in the bottle. That is, it's not ready to drink yet. Buy a couple of bottles and leave them in the cellar to hang out for a while before you open them up to taste again.

FIRM

"The concentrated fruit and bright acidity in the wine help balance out the firm tannins, but I still think we should decant it for an hour to see if it helps them soften up."

STIFF ... as a board. Or like a cocktail: strong. Basically an alternative way of saying that the tannins feel firm; they're very noticeable and unyielding.

"The tannins on this young Xinomavro feel quite stiff; they dominate the palate and overtake the fruit."

Imagine taking a sip of wine and having it cling to your palate like a desperately codependent ex. Like a slightly more intense version of "firm" or "stiff," it's most often used to describe high-tannin reds. Sometimes, though, a white wine with high acidity and intense minerality or pithiness (think the bitter part of citrus zest) can give a similar impression.

GRIPPY

"Tons of beautiful black fruit in this northern Rhône Syrah, but it feels very grippy on the palate. I would revisit the wine in a couple years to let the tannins mellow out and get to a better spot."

CHEWY

Use this term to describe red wines—typically young and fuller bodied—with big tannins that make you feel as though you need to chew air to help release their grip on the inside of your mouth. Expect to notice this in wines made from grapes such as Nebbiolo, Cabernet Sauvignon, Syrah, Sangiovese, Mourvèdre, Petite Sirah, Aglianico, and Tempranillo. Like "firm" wines, these often benefit from decanting or might be best to revisit after they've had some more time to age in the bottle. They're also the kinds of wines that are great to enjoy with hearty, rich, protein-forward dishes that won't be overwhelmed by the tannins.

DRINKING GAME ALERT!

Low-Tannin vs. High-Tannin Wine

For this one, pour yourself a glass of Barbera and a glass of Nebbiolo, two red grapes from the northwestern Italian region of Piedmont with completely

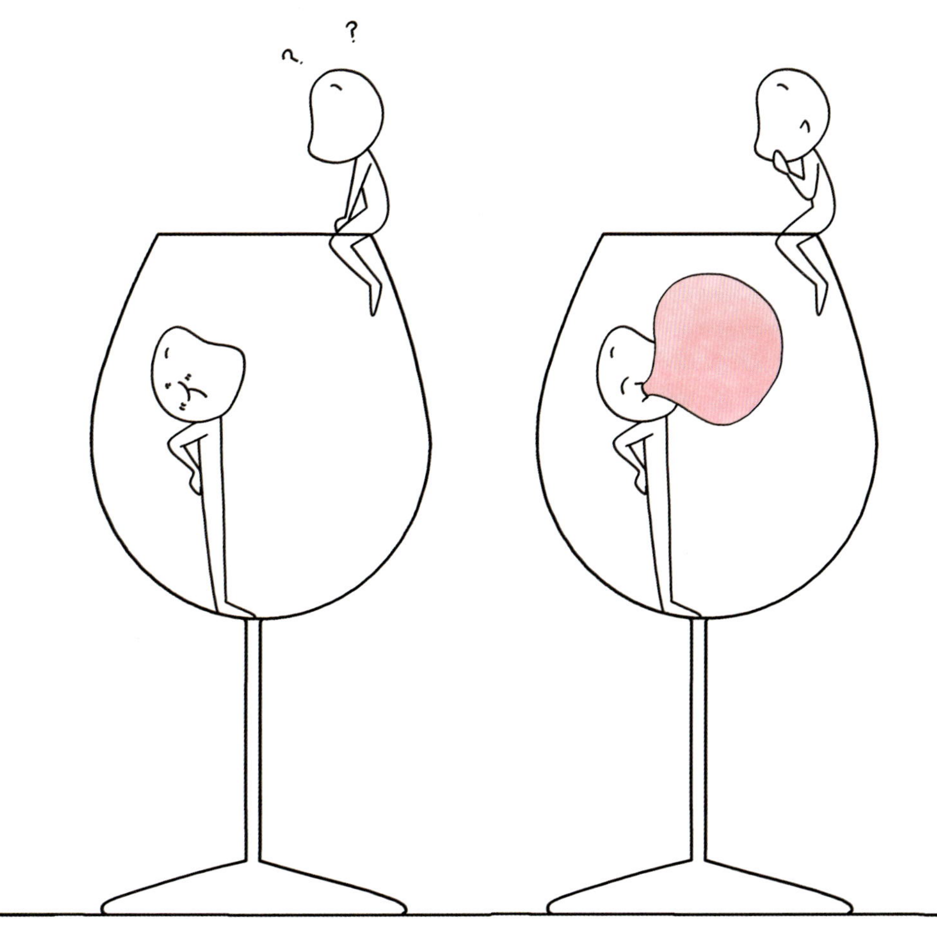

"Damn, those are some chewy tannins. I think the wine will be good with the steak, but I don't know that I'd want more than a glass without food."

different tannic structures. Notice how the Barbera passes over your tongue smoothly and easily; there's very little friction in the texture. Then take a sip of the Nebbiolo and feel the way the wine pulls at your gums and palate. The inside of your mouth likely feels a bit dry, as if it had been hanging open for a few minutes.

7

How Ya Holdin' Up?

Talking About Condition

One of the key things to remember about wine is
that, like us, it has a life cycle. From the moment
it is made to the moment you pop the cork, it's
constantly changing and evolving. The point at
which you open a bottle will provide a snapshot of
where that wine is in its cycle. How it tastes today
is different from how it will taste in six months
or two years from now. And once it's opened, the
clock on the remainder of that wine's lifespan is
on double speed; you have only a limited amount
of time (a couple days, max) before it becomes
oxidized. RIP.

This chapter covers words related to wine's ageability (its potential to improve and develop complexity with time) that can help you express your assessment of where a wine is in its life cycle when you taste it. Does it feel as though it's at its peak and drinking well or as though it's not quite mature yet because you started the party a little too early? If you did open a wine that benefits from aging a bit prematurely, all good; a technique called "decanting" can usually help, and we'll talk about that, too.

Understandably, if you're just getting into wine (or even if you have been for a while), knowing when and how to use these words can be difficult. Don't stress, and certainly don't let it hold you back from trying. The more you drink and taste, the more you talk about wine with people, the more comfortable you'll become and the words will start to flow.

When your bottle is giving restaurant-in-its-prime energy: The kitchen is prepped, the front-of-house staff is trained and eager to go, the reservation book is full, the dining room is looking on point … it's ready to serve. Basically, it's a way of saying "I think this wine is drinking really well right now."

It's particularly useful when talking about older bottles (think $$$ price point) and wines made from grapes that benefit from aging (e.g., Pinot Noir, Cabernet Sauvignon, and Nebbiolo for red; Riesling, Burgundy Chardonnay, and Chenin Blanc for white), which can vary significantly in profile and peak drinkability depending on what point in their life cycle you open them. (Although no one's going to—or *should*—stop you from saying it anytime you want to express that you're just really into the particular bottle you're drinking.)

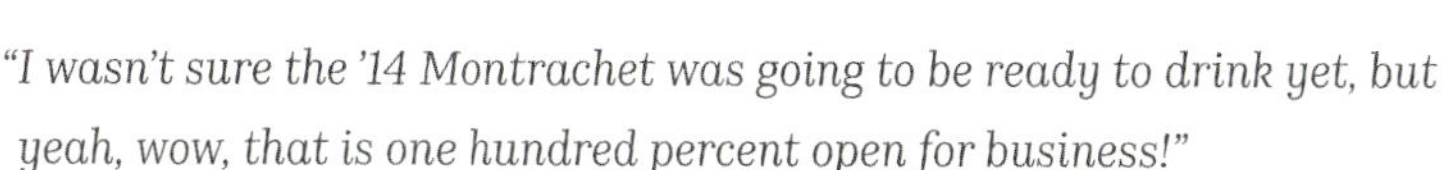

"I wasn't sure the '14 Montrachet was going to be ready to drink yet, but yeah, wow, that is one hundred percent open for business!"

IN A GREAT SPOT

We all have an age that we look back on and think, "Damn, when I was x, I was *peak* me. Like, I really had it all going on." Or maybe you haven't hit yours yet, but you know it's coming. (It is, I promise!) Because we all have one. Or more than one. Use this term when you taste a wine and think that it's at its "living its best life" stage.

"The '06 is in a great spot right now, but the '10 definitely still needs to be laid down for a bit."

When the wine comes out of the bottle like "It's karaoke night, and I am here to *slay.*" It's belting into the mic, it's hitting those high notes, it's working the crowd, and it's walking away with a record contract, baby. It's lively, it has presence, everything is in harmony, and you're in the front row, loving it. The term is most often used to describe the overall impression of a wine, but it can also be used in reference to a specific quality, such as the fruit.

"The fruit is really singing! Cherry, rhubarb, fig…"

CLOSED

The wine equivalent of getting to the store only to find that the lights are off, the door is locked, and no one's there. "Thanks for stopping by, but now's not a good time! Please come back again and visit us later." In a nutshell: the opposite of "open for business."

Usually, if the aroma and flavor of a wine are "quiet" or "muted," it's an indication that it is closed—as though it doesn't have much to say at the moment. It likely needs air (pour it into a decanter) and/or more time to age in the bottle before it finds its voice. The term is often used for wines that typically benefit from aging—think Barolos and Brunellos, high-end Burgundies, red Bordeaux, Priorats—but have been opened too young.

"I was hoping that this Brunello would be open for business, but it still feels closed. The palate is flat and the nose is pretty muted, only faint hints of cherry and tobacco coming through."

Similar to "closed"; the wine's flavor profile is not very expressive or it's overpowered by high levels of tannin, acidity, and/or alcohol—but with more of an implied confidence that the wine will open up relatively quickly with time and air. It's like when you drag that friend who *hates* going out to a party. At first they're stiff, shy, hiding awkwardly in the corner, not talking to anyone. But when you check back a little while (and several glasses of wine) later, they're all loosened up, chitchatting away, having a grand old time with everyone. Popular variations on this descriptor include "tightly wound," "tightly coiled," and "tightly knit."

TIGHT

"This Burgundy Pinot Noir still feels a bit tight, but it's opened up since we opened it half an hour ago. I think that after another thirty minutes in the decanter, those savory forest floor aromas will start to shine and the firmness will smooth out."

NEEDS TIME TO X

Use the following "Needs time to" expressions when talking about:

- Older bottles (They need time to rub the sleep out of their post-hibernation eyes! The wine's been lying dormant in there for a while.)

- Fuller-bodied whites and reds

- Reds with harsh tannins

- Wines that smell reduced, a word that means they are a little stinky from having been made in an anaerobic (oxygen-free) environment such as a stainless-steel tank

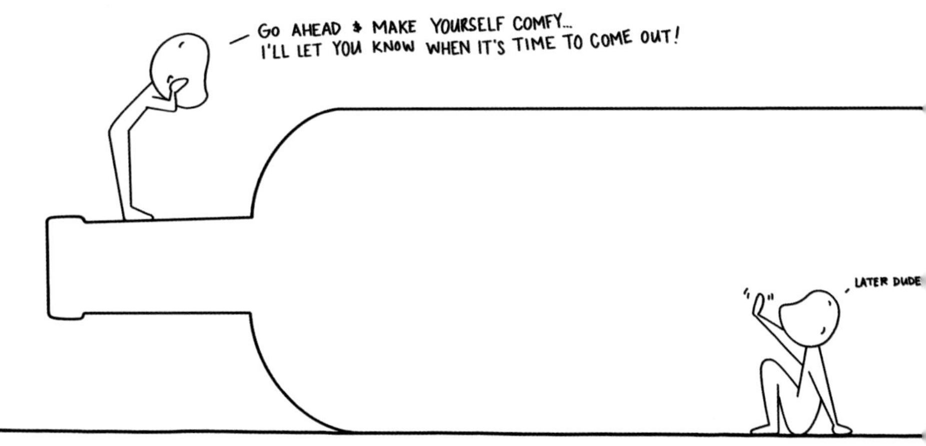

"This doesn't quite feel ready to drink yet; it needs more time in bottle for sure. I would put the other two bottles you have in the cellar and revisit them in a couple years."

Needs more time in bottle/ needs time to be laid down

When you've opened a bottle before it's ready. No amount of decanting or swirling the wine in your glass will help. It's not open for business. Not in a great spot. Obviously, you can still drink it; it's not flawed per se—and it's open, might as well— but you're acknowledging that it doesn't quite meet your expectations. Admittedly, this can be difficult to discern. But any wine on a restaurant list should be ready to drink, and you should expect that most bottles available for retail sale are good to go, too. However, a good bottle shop might have some selections they'd recommend that you cellar (hold on to and not open for a while), in which case, buy a couple of bottles and try them after different periods of time.

Needs time to open up

When you first taste a wine and feel that it's acting a little shy, like the office newbie at their first company happy hour before they've had any liquid courage. It'll get there and reveal its personality to you eventually, but it's just not ready yet.

"The nose is pretty muted; definitely needs some time to open up."

Needs time to unfurl

Like "Needs time to open up" but sultry.

*"This wine needed a couple hours in the decanter to unfurl before it really
started to shine."*

Needs time to breathe

Stand back, people! Stand back! Let's give the wine some air! This is a frequent tasting-notes partner with "Needs time to open up." If you're saying that a wine needs to "open up," you're saying that it needs to breathe; pour the bottle into a decanter and/or give the wine in your glass a few vigorous swirls. See if it loosens up— improves, becomes more interesting, evolves— with some air and time.

"Whoa, those are some grippy tannins! Let's try decanting it, because it needs to breathe and open up."

TOTALLY DIFFERENT ANIMAL ON/AFTER

How you would describe a wine whose character has significantly changed and evolved from when you first opened it and tasted it. This will often come up with wines that initially feel "tight" or "closed" and require aeration to open up.

"I can't believe the aromas coming off this now—it was super tightly coiled at first, but it's a totally different animal after three hours in the decanter."

The Five W's and One H of Decanting

Your "who," "what," "where," "when," "why," and "how" guide to decanting wine. What = What does "decanting" mean? Who = Which wines should be decanted? Where = Some things to keep in mind when choosing a decanter (aka where your wine is being transferred into). Why = Reasons to decant. When (not to) = When you *shouldn't* decant. How = A step-by-step guide to getting 'er done.

What

Transferring the wine out of its bottle and into another serving vessel to oxygenate for a period of time before pouring it into a glass.

Who

Most often, high-quality red wines that are designed for aging that you want to open before they're fully in a great spot and open for business. But also older (middle-aged-plus) high-quality red wines, some high-quality, fuller-bodied, oaked whites, and wines that smell reduced.

Where

A range of styles in a range of price points exists, but generally, the standard decanter is made from glass with a wide-ish bowl-shaped base and narrow neck. Some design-related things to consider:

- The narrower the decanter, the slower the rate of oxygenation.

- A wider, larger base means that more of the wine's surface area is exposed to oxygen, so it will aerate faster.

- An angled spout is easier to pour from.

- If you find fingerprints triggering, the "duck"-style decanter features a handle.

- It's your money and you're the one who's going to be looking at it on the table, so you should enjoy the shape and design. But in my humble opinion, practically speaking, the showboaty ones are mainly just for showboating. Also, cleaning those high-fashion decanters can be a pain in the ass.

Why

The two main reasons:

1. **To aerate the wine.**

   - If it's meant to age but you want to open it before it's fully mature, the interaction with the air should help it wake up and fast-forward its evolution, showing how it would be at its peak had it aged naturally. It's basically the equivalent of having a way to get soup-on-day-three flavor (everyone knows that soup tastes better after a couple days) without having to wait three days.

   - It helps soften tannins and enhance aroma.

   - It can help stinky "reduced" aromas blow off from wines made in anaerobic environments.

2. **To remove sediment.**

   - Bottles of older red wines will likely contain sediment, those grainy particles that are a naturally occurring by-product when wine is made and aged. Consuming sediment isn't going to hurt you, but it's far from pleasant (like eating greens that are gritty because they haven't been properly washed).

A couple more reasons:

- You accidentally broke the cork and had to push the remaining half into the bottle. Oops! But honestly, no biggie. Quickly pour that wine into a decanter; no one will be the wiser.

- You feel that your wine is too cold and you want to warm it.

- You like the presentation better. Maybe the bottle label is all scuffed or you just think it looks classier. You do you.

When (Not to)

Honestly, most wine doesn't *need* to be decanted because it's ready to drink as is. Figuring out if and how much air your wine needs is a complicated, and delicate dance. Decanting a suuuuuuper old bottle that's fragile and on its way over the hill could be the thing that sends it tumbling down. If you're worried about this, it's best to avoid decanting.

Anyone who's ever had to throw out half-full cans of flat beer the day after a party knows that air and bubbles are not the best of friends. So you can probably avoid decanting your bubbs, too—although there are some strong advocates for decanting Champagne.

How

If it's a younger wine and you're not worried about sediment: Quickly smell and/or taste the wine (to make sure it's not corked), then pick up the bottle in one hand and hold the decanter in the other, tilted at a slight angle. Tip the bottle to meet the spout of the decanter and start pouring. Slowly and gradually angle your pouring arm up (elbow toward the sky), allowing the wine to flow in until it's all transferred.

DRINKING GAME ALERT!

Getting Your Wine to Loosen Up

For this game, we're going to try to see the impact that air and time have on a wine. You can try this with any wine, but for results that will hopefully be more obvious, you're going to pick up a young vintage (two to three years old, tops) of a full-bodied, medium-to-high-tannin red, something like a Tuscan Sangiovese (Chianti Classico or Brunello di Montalcino if you're feelin' fancy), a Syrah from France's northern Rhône Valley, or a Cabernet Sauvignon. Open the bottle,

If it's an older wine and you're decanting for sediment: Stand the unopened bottle upright on the counter for at least an hour. (Wine bottles should be kept on their side when you're storing them, so standing a bottle upright helps the sediment settle at the bottom.)

When you're ready to pop the cork, you'll follow the same steps as previously described, but with a bright light positioned to shine through the shoulders and neck of the bottle (so you can see the sediment). The flashlight on your phone is perfect for this; just set the phone face down on the counter and hold the bottle in your dominant hand over the light. (Make sure not to blind yourself!) Then start pouring the wine into the decanter. When the bottle is close to empty and you start to see a stream of dark, powdery haze, pull the bottle back upright away from the decanter.

pour yourself a taste, then give the wine a sniff and sip right away. How prominent are the aromas? Do the tannins feel really intense and grippy? Decant the wine, and taste it again after about thirty to forty-five minutes. How do the tannins feel now? A little softer and smoother? What about the aroma? Anything new popping out that you didn't notice before? Pour one glass from the decanter, set it aside, and try it again after about two hours. How are those tannins feeling now? Have they loosened up even more? What about the weight of the wine? Does it feel a little rounder? And let's go back to the aroma and flavor: Is it more expressive, less expressive, or kind of the same?

8

What a Character

Talking About Personality

This is going to date me, but remember back when *Sex and the City* was really big and you and your friends would play the "Who is which character?" game? So-and-so was the "Charlotte" because she was a little more prim and goody-two-shoes traditional. Whoever was the cynical, snarky, smarty-pants one was the "Miranda." The confident, sexy one who got all the attention was the "Samantha," and the popular one who was creative and obsessed with fashion was, of course, the "Carrie."

Funnily enough, we do something kind of similar when describing wine. Sometimes, instead of calling out a series of qualities of a given wine, such as "It has a ton of rich fruit, really big tannins, big alcohol, and softer acidity," we'll use a personality type descriptor that sums it right up. You know, captures the vibe in a nice, concise, one-word package, kind of like a code word. In the case of that example, that word would be "muscular." In the next section, we'll get into the many personality types you can encounter in wine.

FRIENDLY AND APPROACHABLE

When your wine is giving golden retriever energy: easy to drink, easy to like, not overly complex or serious. Wines that fall into the category of "crushable" or "porch pounder" are generally described this way.

"Pinot Grigio is definitely one of the most friendly and approachable white wines—it's dry and crisp, but the acidity isn't too intense, pleasant fruit notes, nothing too loud."

Like a cheerleader: nice, bright, spirit-fingers
bubbly, with lots of energy and youthful
freshness.

PEPPY

*"This Greek white is super peppy! The bright, salty citrus and melon notes
are bouncing around my palate with tons of enthusiasm."*

CRUSH-ABLE

When the wine is so tasty and easy to drink it feels as though you could knock it back as fast as a college bro can take down a sixer of Coors Light.

The term is usually used in reference to a lighter-bodied wine with bright acidity, lower alcohol, and low tannins (if it's a red), or a non-Champagne sparkling. And probably not a wine that's too spendy (because why would you want to chug a bottle that cost you more than $20?). Which is not to say that calling a wine "crushable" means that it's low quality; it can be a well-made wine from a great producer, it's just that the style is more fun and easy and the wine doesn't take itself too seriously.

The word could also be used to express that you really enjoy the wine. Like "Damn, that's so good I could crush that bottle waaaaay too fast."

"We might need to get more than one of those bottles. I've had it before, and it's suuuuuuper crushable."

The kind of wine that flows freely when you're sitting out on the porch and gossiping with your bestie. It's not about the wine. The wine may be good, but it is not the point. It's just the fuel for the piping hot tea that's being spilled. Think light, friendly whites such as Pinot Grigio, Vinho Verde, and Txakolina; chillable light reds such as Gamay and Frappato; and most rosés.

PORCH POUNDER

"What wine do you want to bring to the party tonight? I'm thinking we just need a couple porch pounders, something easy."

GLOU-GLOU Like "crushable" but cooler, because, you know... it's French. It's onomatopoeia for the glug-glug sound you'd hear when pouring yourself that big glass of wine you *need* at the end of a long day. Or chugging the wine straight from the bottle (please, we know you're not above it) if it was a really, *really* long day. If you want to fit in at a natural wine bar or bottle shop, toss this word into your conversation. The expression reemerged and really started to gain traction in the early 2000s as a way to describe the natural wines of Beaujolais that helped kick-start the current obsession with that style of wine. The buzzword has essentially become emblematic of natural wine's fun, free-spirited, anti-snob vibe.

"I'm obsessed with this Beaujy—superbright fruit, a little funky, totally glou-glou."

If "crushable" and "porch pounder" wines give party school vibes, cerebral wines are repping the Ivy League. Use this term when a wine feels complex and layered and not immediately easy to understand, but in an intriguing way. There's a lot there for you to think about and notice, and with every sip something new and interesting is revealed.

Note: Do not think of this term as exclusive to expensive wine! News flash: Just because you paid more for a bottle does not guarantee that it is going to be good (or that you'll like it). Okay, fine, sure—the chances that you're going to find a "cerebral" wine in the bargain bin at the liquor mart are probably pretty slim. But the point is that there are plenty of complex, intriguing, make-you-stop-and-think wines that are not at the break-the-bank price point.

CEREBRAL

"This wine is incredibly cerebral. I'm really trying to take my time with this glass because there's so much going on and it keeps evolving as it unfurls."

LAYERED

You know, like what Shrek said about ogres and onions. There's a lot to discover beyond the surface.

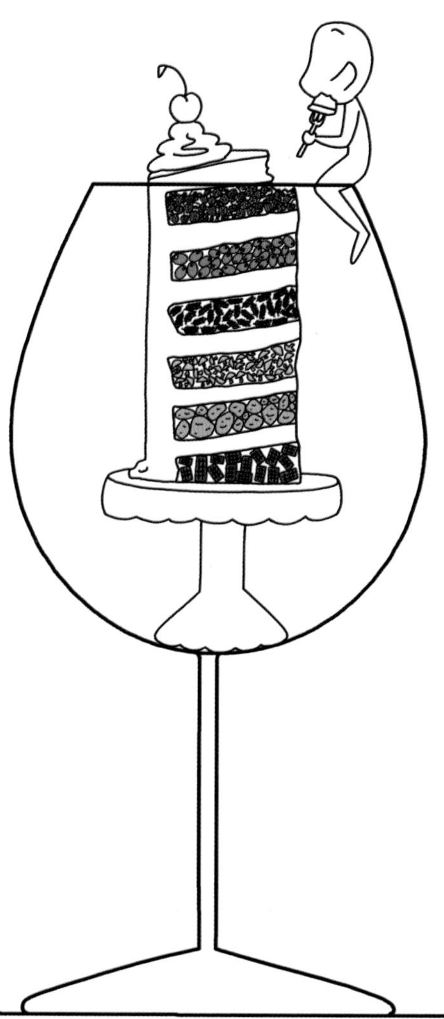

"I find this Syrah to be beautifully layered, with notes of ripe black cherry and blackberry up front, leading the way to hints of chocolate, lavender, and savory umami undertones."

When your wine is showing off one or more of its characteristics—usually its fruit profile—in a not-at-all-subtle kind of way. If it's showing off *everything* at once—big fruit, big tannins, big body, big alcohol—that's when you could take it a step further and call it "muscular." "Flexing" could also be used to express that you're impressed with a wine's overall presentation. Like, what it's about, what it's serving up, you're into it. Please and thank you.

FLEXING

"The fruit in this Primitivo sure is flexing! Tons of ripe, lush, juicy blackberry and plum smacking you in the face."

SHY

A synonym of "quiet" and "restrained" or even "tight." What you might say when a wine's aromas and flavors are acting timid. They're peeking out and waving "Hi" from behind the corner; you notice them, they're in the room, but they're not exactly rushing over excitedly to give you a big hug.

"There's some pretty fruit there on the nose, but it feels a bit shy at the moment; it's hard to pick up on."

Like a prima ballerina in wine form: delicate, graceful, poised, ethereal, captivating. This term is generally used for lighter-to-medium-bodied wines with lively acidity, not-too-in-your-face tannins, and a more demure fruit profile.

ELEGANT

"This Barbaresco is such a restrained and elegant expression of Nebbiolo. The interplay between the fruit and savory notes … the silky texture of the fine-grained tannins on the palate … the vibrant, lively acidity, it's all so balanced and drinks with incredible finesse."

AWKWARD Remember yourself in middle school? (I know, I'd rather not, either.) Slouchy, gangly, clumsy, not quite comfortable in your own skin, imbalanced. It's like that in a wine. The wine gives an overall impression of being kind of disjointed and out of whack.

"This Cabernet Sauvignon feels a bit awkward, I think because it's still so young. The oak and tannins are overpowering the fruit; it needs some time in bottle to settle into itself."

Picture going out for the most over-the-top meal: oysters and caviar … pâté de foie gras and truffles … butter-poached lobster and wagyu sirloin. An opulent wine delivers a sensory extravaganza, a celebration of richness and decadence. It's definitely extra, yet it doesn't leave you feeling gross. It retains an element of elegance and refinement; there's still balance. The term can be applied to a red or white wine, usually medium to full bodied and fruit forward, with a complex aroma and flavor profile—and, more than likely, on the expensive end of the price spectrum. For reds, think Napa Valley Cabernet Sauvignon, a high-quality Shiraz from Barossa Valley in South Australia, or Amarone from Valpolicella in northeastern Italy. For whites, a Chardonnay from a prestige growing region in Burgundy (e.g., Montrachet), Alsatian Gewürztraminer, or Viognier from Condrieu in France's Rhône Valley.

"I find the opulence of an Amarone so completely seductive—super ripe, rich, and velvety on the palate, with intriguing notes of dried fig, brandied cherry, dark chocolate, and worn leather."

FLAMBOYANT

At the same restaurant as "opulent" but a couple tables over. A loud "Look at me! Look at me!" group with their phones out, flashlights on, recording everything live for the 'gram. Very brazen in its play to capture your attention; shoving handfuls of fruit in your face. Use this term when you taste a wine and notice that it has a big, ripe, excessively flashy fruit profile that dominates the supporting characteristics. It can be used as a bit of a dig, especially if you're into leaner, more restrained wines, but as ever, whether you like it or not depends on the style of wine you like!

"This style of Malbec is a little too flamboyant for me—the fruit feels excessively concentrated, so it reads a bit heavy on the palate. I'm missing that jolt of acidity or some tannic framework."

That opulent meal but with circa Roman Empire HEDONISTIC energy. Overly indulgent in a way that feels kinda wrong. But also right. Probably more of a special occasion kind of wine as opposed to something you're going to drink every night (unless maybe you're a finance or tech bro with one hell of an expense account).

"This 2008 Auslese Riesling is pure hedonism—the layers of ripe, juicy nectarine and honeyed peaches are so well balanced with that electric hit of lime zesty acidity and subtle hint of petrol. Round and mouth coating, with a finish that keeps going for days."

BIG/ MASSIVE

A wine with a personality that fills the whole room. (And by "room," I mean your nose and palate.) Like "opulent" or "hedonistic" but probably more commonly used for everyday kinds of wines as opposed to wines that fall into the special occasion category. The wine has a fuller body and texture, a bigger structure, and a bigger fruit profile (usually) but lacks sexiness; it's not dripping in diamonds or wrapped in fur.

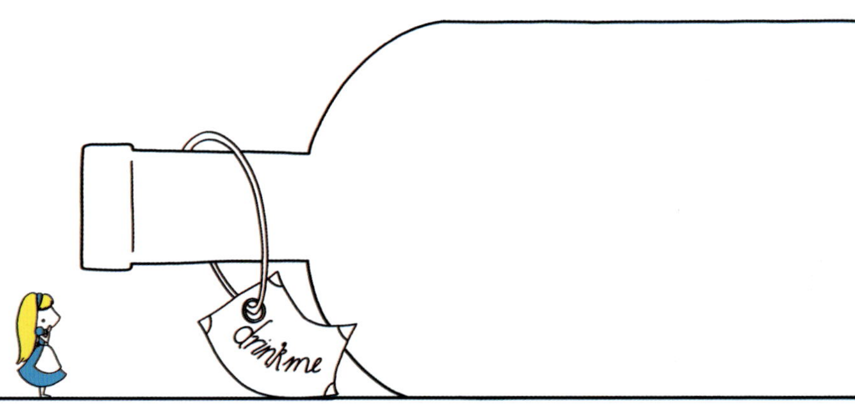

"That Petit Sirah from Napa is massive! Tons of mouth-coating, inky dark berry fruit bursting on the palate. Superrich and full bodied with firm tannins. It's got presence, that's for sure."

What you might say when a wine has a "giving" personality, like a grandma who *must* feed you and just keeps putting more and more food onto your plate. "Here, have a snack. Take seconds. Take some leftovers. And don't you dare think about getting up from this table without trying my homemade pie!" The wine's characteristics fall more onto the full, rich, and round side. The term is frequently used in reference to a wine's fruit profile, similar to "fruit forward," meaning that the fruit flavors are concentrated and at the forefront. But it can also be used to describe other qualities about the wine, such as its acidity or texture. Or, if it's one or more of the above, you might describe it as an overall personality assessment.

GENEROUS

"This Napa Chardonnay feels incredibly generous on the palate, with a round, creamy texture and notes of baked apple pie, warm spices, and buttery brioche."

RESTRAINED The equivalent of a wine being at an all-you-can-eat buffet but having the self-control to go for only one plate. It's how you would describe a wine that is typically known for being big, rich, or overly indulgent but that is made in a more delicate, subdued style.

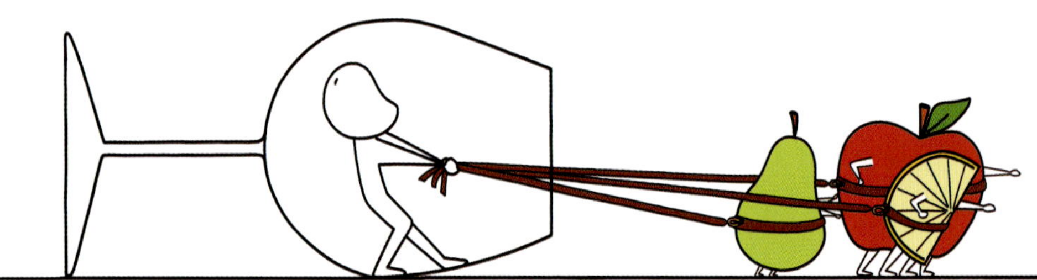

"Normally a Pinotage is too big and muscular for me, but this one actually feels quite elegant and restrained!"

A popular blanket term used to describe a wine with a flavor profile that's a little … "different," like Ally Sheedy's character in *The Breakfast Club* or Janis Ian in *Mean Girls* vibes. This trait can be polarizing and is probably not for everyone; it's the opposite of friendly and easy to understand. Think pungent, earthy, stinky (or barnyardy), savory, and/or sour. The term is frequently used to describe natural wines.

"The aroma of this skin-contact Pinot Gris is definitely a little funky. I like it! A bit of a peach kombucha mixed with a roasted almond, ginger, and potting soil vibe."

POLISHED

Picture a car that's been immaculately detailed: shiny, smooth, sleek. So fresh and so clean, clean. Classy AF energy for daaaays. That's more or less the experience of drinking a "polished" wine: It feels refined, balanced, and elegant, with a smooth texture and a long finish. It sails across the palate. Picture perfect and expen$$$ive. Every component is in check, not a single proverbial hair is out of place. The term is probably more often used positively, but it could also be used as a negative if someone's trying to say that it feels overproduced and too squeaky clean. It really depends on your personal preference.

"This Rioja Riserva feels impeccably polished: velvety on the palate, with beautifully integrated aromas of red cherry, plum, dried tobacco, and cedar. The acidity is still driving and carries the fruit through a long, elegant finish. You can tell this is a really skillfully made wine."

RUSTIC

When the vibe of the wine is more hidden-gem, hole-in-the-wall family restaurant than three-star Michelin with white tablecloths and assembled-with-tweezers dishes. It's the restaurant in season one of *The Bear* versus the one in season two. Admittedly, it's not the easiest quality to identify in a wine because there's no checklist of things that make it so. Again, whether this is a positive or a negative will depend on the perspective of the taster. It's subjective. But generally speaking, the term works well as a foil for wines that are very "produced" and flashy. They tend to be a little rougher around the edges, unpretentious, you know, very "I'm not perfect and I don't want to be, and that's okay."

"This is exactly what I want out of a Chianti—rustic in such a charming way. The tannins are a little dusty, there's a slight grip there with some snappy acidity to match. Tons of savory notes exploding out of the glass. It just feels soulful, like a bowl of Nonna's bolognese."

What Is Natural Wine?

Trying to answer the question "What is natural wine?" in a sound bite-sized sidebar is like trying to recap seasons one to ten of your favorite TV show fifteen minutes before season eleven is about to start. If you're truly curious about this very interesting (I think) topic, it's worth finding an entire book about it—there are great ones out there—and go for the deep dive, the whole series binge.

The big complicating factor is that there is no clear-cut, everyone-agrees-upon-this definition of what makes a natural wine a natural wine. Th interpretation of the practice is different from winemaker to winemaker. There is no regulating body that gives wineries a sticker or label stamp to certify that they are so, and whether or not there should be is a whole other debate. The point is, it's fuzzy territory, especially now that natural wines have become so trendy and buzzy and cool-kid beloved.

But for our purposes, here's the long and the short of it: It's wine made with minimal to no intervention from the winemaker at every step of the process, from vineyard to glass. The goal is to let the varietal, the terroir, the vintage, and other factors shine through on their own without being manipulated by technology or additives. It's basically wine with no makeup on.

Generally speaking, this is some of what you can expect from wines that identify as natural:

- Organic or biodynamic farming practices.

- Hand-harvested grapes.

- From smaller family-owned wineries with smaller production volume.

- No additions or heavy manipulation in the winery (only native yeast is used for fermentation; no color or flavor additives; no added sugar).

- Bottled unfined and unfiltered (expect some of them to be cloudy) and with minimal to no added sulfites.

- The use of lesser-known grape varietals and unique experimental techniques.

- Lower alcohol content.

- *Lots* of acidity.

- Lighter to medium body in terms of weight (even wines made from fuller-bodied grapes seem to present at the lighter end of their spectrum).

- The words "funky," "savory," and/or "barnyard" will most likely come up in a description.

- Some really cool, super fun, super creative label design and cheeky wordplay in the name. (Don't let anyone judge you for having a cool label influence you to buy a wine. The producer chose to make it look cool for a reason.)

TENSION

Tension in your relationship or at work? Eek, bad, no, thank you. In wine? Quite the opposite; it's a positive—though it's another one of those words that is difficult to pinpoint definition-wise because it means different things to different tasters. Some use it to describe the way a wine's flavors or characteristics interact with one another; when it feels as though two or more elements are playing tug-of-war on your palate, pulling your attention back and forth in an exciting and engaging way: fruit vs. minerality or texture vs. weight, for example. Others might use the word as they would "energy," "lively," or "nervy," usually as a result of the wine having a high acidity level.

"The tension between the citrusy acidity and cool mineral tones in this Sardinian Vermentino adds a nice complexity."

Like that one kid from high school who was in every club and on every committee, played every sport, had about ten superlatives under their yearbook photo, *and* managed to keep a 4.0 GPA. It's a compliment, a way of expressing that you really like the wine and think it's practically perfect in every way (almost annoyingly so). Of course, what qualifies it to achieve overachiever status is personal to you and depends on what you like and look for in a wine.

*"Holy sh*t, can we talk about that 2004 Barolo? What an absolute overachiever."*

OVER-DELIVERS

How you would describe a wine that exceeds your expectations. It's like when you hear that yet another reality star is "following their lifelong passion for music" (groan). Except then you listen to the new single, and *gasp!* it's actually kind of a bop and you're low-key obsessed. Often the term is used in relation to something else in order to give context: price (it's inexpensive, but it doesn't taste cheap); vintage (maybe the wine was produced in a year when a lot of wineries in the area struggled for one reason or another, but this isn't showing it); or region (when the wine comes from a less prestigious region known for making more basic wine, but this tastes as though it has a pedigree).

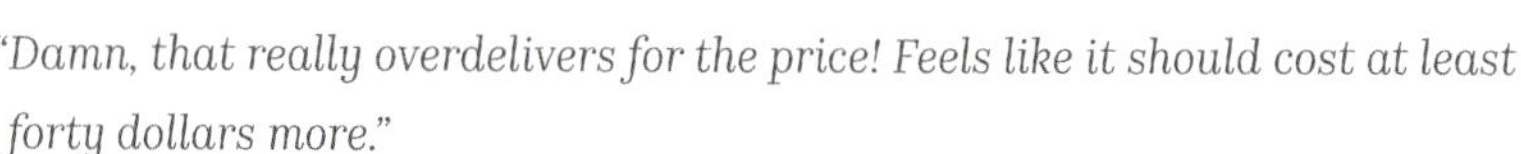

"Damn, that really overdelivers for the price! Feels like it should cost at least forty dollars more."

When you find a wine—or a specific quality of said wine—so incredible, so impactful, so memorable that it stays with you. It's like a ghost, but a friendly one (Casper!) that you are happy to have around and be reminded of. For me, it was a 1997 Alsatian Riesling that *completely* blew my mind, changing my expectations for and understanding of the grape and what it could taste like. It's probably a word that will more often be associated with wines that are more complex, rare, and/or higher end.

HAUNTING

"That 1986 Pomerol we had for Christmas dinner was so beautiful it's still haunting me—it still had incredible subtle power and finesse, and I couldn't get enough of the umami, forest floor notes."

9

Add It to the Burn Book

Talking About Faults and Flaws

Wine can be as imperfect and as fallible as any of us. It can have little not-so-pleasant personality traits that don't do it any favors. It can sometimes not have its shit together; be "too old"; go through experiences or interact with something that turns it for the worse. (This, I should point out, is different from your just not liking something because it's not your personal taste. That's totally fine, but it's not the same as its being technically flawed or faulty, as when it's volatile or corked, for example.)

When the not-quite-right, not-quite-normal thing is minor, it's considered to be a flaw. It's something you notice, but it doesn't dominate, or maybe it dissipates over time. In some cases, you might even *like* the effect the flaw has on the wine, find that it makes it more interesting because there's beauty in imperfection and all that jazz. But if the flaw is severe, if it becomes the wine's entire personality, then it pushes over the line into fault territory. This chapter covers all the so-called wine digs and disses you need to know, but hopefully you won't have to use them all that much!

CORKED

How you would describe a wine that has been affected by 2,4,6-trichloroanisole, aka TCA, aka cork taint, aka the Joker to wine's Batman.

How can you tell if your wine has fallen victim to this formidable foe? Look for disappointment-inducing aromas of musky wet dog, damp newspaper, cardboard that's been left out in the rain, stale old musty dive bar, or dank moldy basement. It's not unsafe to drink, but it's definitely not enjoyable, since any of the wine's other aromas and flavors are completely clobbered by the aforementioned unpleasantness.

Unfortunately, there's no fix for it. You can't decant the stank away; you just have to take the L and move on. In a restaurant you can point it out to your server or sommelier and get a replacement, and a good bottle shop should do the same if you recork the bottle and take it back.

It should be obvious, but it's worth mentioning: This fault occurs only in wines with cork closures, so you can leave it off the list of potential worries about any screw cap, synthetic cork, or glass closure wines.

"Damn, I'm so disappointed that the wine ended up being corked! I've been holding on to it in my cellar for a while, waiting to taste it with you."

Not a euphemism for an attack move in a *Star Wars* battle scene but the way you would describe a wine that has been damaged by UV light. Light and wine are not friends, which is why wine bottles are often made of green or amber glass and why it's recommended that you store your wine someplace dark, such as a basement. Sparkling wines and lighter, more delicate whites and rosés are most susceptible to this flaw, especially when packaged in clear glass bottles. It can dull fruit aromas and produce icky smells such as dank damp laundry, rotten eggs, and sewage.

"Eek, the rosé might be a victim of light strike—smells a little rotten eggy on the nose. Was it out by the window for a while or something?"

MADERIZED   What you would call a wine that has been damaged by exposure to heat. Heat and wine are also not friends. Wine is *not* a fun-in-the-sun, tropical vacation kind of girlie. It doesn't like hanging out on your countertop next to the stove or sitting in the trunk of your car on a hot summer day while you run errands.

A red wine that's overheated has fruit flavors that taste stewed or cooked; whites have an unpleasant roasted-nut quality and a brownish tinge. Noticing that the cork has started to push out of the bottle before you open it can be a clue that the wine has maderized.

Long story short: Keep your wine away from areas above 70°F; ideally, it should be stored between about 53° and 59°F.

"You might want to move your wine rack. I think the bottles might be getting too much heat and sun, because this wine feels a bit maderized; the fruit tastes like it's been stewed, and the color's a tad brownish."

How you'd describe a wine that's had too much exposure to air. Like if you opened a bottle of wine and didn't finish it (first of all, that's impressive) and came back for that last glass five or more days later; that's what "oxidized" looks and tastes like. The color starts to go brownish, and the flavor turns stale, dull, and vinegary.

OXIDIZED/ OXIDATION

Wine is confusing, isn't it fun?

At some point, you might hear someone describe a wine as having been made in an "oxidative" style. This means it was intentionally and in a controlled way exposed to a higher amount of oxygen during the winemaking process, the goal being to develop complexity by coaxing out dried fruit, nutty, yeasty, and/ or savory notes. Probably the easiest way to think about the difference between oxidative and oxidized is like the difference between dry- aging a steak and forgetting a steak on the countertop overnight. If you're curious about oxidative style wines, check out whites (Chardonnay and Savagnin) from France's Jura region or sherries from Spain.

"*I think we need to dump the rest of this wine we opened a couple days ago. It's oxidized; the flavor's totally gone.*"

REDUCED/ REDUCTION

If oxidation is what happens when you give your wine too much air, reduction is the flip side of the coin, the result of a wine's *lack* of exposure to oxygen during the winemaking process. Taken to an extreme, this can result in a wine that smells like a bad high school prank—as if someone hit your house with rotten eggs and garbage and then burned rubber peeling off in the getaway car.

The good news is that if you notice that your wine smells reduced, you can try giving it a little air shock therapy by pouring it into a decanter and/or giving it a couple aggressive swirls in a glass to help those pinch-your-nose flavors "blow off" (aka fade away).

Wine is confusing, isn't it fun?
In the spirit of "there can be beauty in flaws" (see also "Volatile acidity" and "Brettanomyces"), it's important to note that reduction isn't always or necessarily a bad thing. When done in a balanced, measured way, reductive winemaking can help preserve a wine's fresh fruit aromas and add a layer of depth with an appealing flinty or smoky note. Chardonnays from Burgundy and Chenin Blancs from the Loire Valley can be great examples of reductive winemaking done right.

"The wine was smelling a bit reduced, so I gave it a quick decant, and now it seems like it's blown off. The pretty citrus and herbal notes are coming through, and that stinky burnt rubber thing is gone."

"VA" or "volatile" for short; this is what you would call it if your wine has a noticeable amount of acetic acid, i.e., it smells like vinegar or nail polish remover.

VOLATILE ACIDITY

This is another polarizing characteristic. When it's overdone, it can make a wine feel burn-your-nose-hairs sour. Done well (and whatever "well" means depends on your personal preferences), a little VA can help give it a high-toned brightness, what wine peeps call a "lifted" quality—as if the VA was that extra little bit of oomph needed to hold the aromas up and show them off, big-lift move in *Dirty Dancing* style. If you're into natural wines, you probably appreciate some VA.

"The Cabernet Franc is a little volatile, but on the palate it really lifts the sour cherry and cranberry notes and gives it a nice brightness and refreshing quality."

BRET-TANOMYCES

"*Brett*" for short, it's the yeast responsible for making your wine smell as though it was raised in a horse barn, rolling around in manurey hay and sidling up to sweaty saddles. If you ever hear someone (probably talking about or drinking natural wine) calling out "barnyard" as a tasting note, it's because of Brett. Its effect is more or less synonymous with "funky," and a common descriptor for wines categorized as "rustic." It can also give off whiffs of Band-Aid. It's *technically* considered a fault, and admittedly, it doesn't paint the most appetizing picture. Like anything, if not managed properly by the winemaker, if the stank is really stanking, it can overpower the other flavors in the glass. But trust me, with the right wine (usually red), in moderate doses, it can add a compelling earthy-spicy-leathery complexity to the profile, kind of like a secret sauce seasoning. See if you can pick up on it in reds from France's Rhône Valley, Loire Valley, and Beaujolais regions; a Sangiovese from Tuscany; or a classic style of California Cabernet.

*"I know **Brett** can be a bit much for some people, but I love the funky, barnyardy quality it brings to this Morgon."*

HOT

When the person you have a crush on describes you as "hot." Amazing. Love it. Whole week made. But when it's used to describe a wine, it does not have the same complimentary effect. It's how you would characterize a wine whose alcohol content feels overwhelmingly high. It makes the wine seem unbalanced because it's all you notice—stinging your nostrils and leaving a burning sensation in the back of your throat.

It's worth noting that the perception of alcohol dissipates over time. So if you taste a wine and it feels a bit hot, get another bottle and try it again after some time (a couple of months; years, even) and see if the alcohol has had a chance to mellow and blend in better with the rest of the wine's components.

"Must have been a warm vintage; it's drinking really hot on the finish."

MESSY

Like a Real Housewife after one (okay, five) too many shots of tequila. All over the place, off balance, not making much sense. Basically, you're saying that the wine's components feel disjointed. Maybe the texture is out of whack with the level of acidity and fruit, and then all of a sudden some unnecessary oaky notes come out of left field? Whatever it is, the equation is not adding up.

"I don't know what is going on with this wine, but it feels super messy—odd candied quality to the fruit, lacking texture, and the oak presence is way too overpowering."

When you taste the wine and it feels as though there's a giant sinkhole in the middle of your palate. You can pick up on some flavor up front when you take a sip and on the finish as you swallow, but oddly (and disappointingly), the flavor intensity drops off in between those two points.

HOLLOW

"I'm missing the usual rich, velvety texture of this Douro red; feels oddly hollow."

OVER THE HILL

How you'd describe a bottle of an older vintage of wine that tastes as though it's past its prime; it peaked before you opened it. It goes back to that life cycle of wine thing. You gotta catch your wine at the right moment. It's as if someone gave you a VHS tape and a PalmPilot for your birthday this year. Like, "What am I supposed to do with these fossils?" It doesn't necessarily mean that the wine tastes "bad," but you know that it might have tasted better at some point. The aroma and flavors seem faded.

It's obviously not something that's easy to determine, especially if you're just starting to explore wine, but even if you're not! There's no perfect formula for how long to age a given wine and when to drink it. But it helps if you've drunk that wine or wines from that producer or region several times before so at least you're familiar with what to expect.

Some signs that your wine might be over the hill are:

- *The cork is super dry and crumbly.*

- *The wine looks and smells oxidized (brownish, with pronounced vinegary and nutty aromas).*

- *There's a little unexpected fizz or cloudiness in the liquid.*

- *You give it time to open up, but it's still not giving the standing ovation performance you were hoping for.*

"I might have waited too long to open this red. Feels like it's over the hill. It's showing signs of oxidation, and it hasn't really improved much after decanting."

Drinking a great wine should feel like listening to a symphony: complex and layered with all of its various elements working in concert. If it's playing only one note of one instrument, that sensation is simply not going to be achieved. Basically, you're calling the wine … basic. Only one quality or characteristic stands out, making it feel unbalanced and boring.

ONE NOTE

"Was super excited to open this, but sadly it's totally one note."

DEAD

If "over the hill" is like saying "This wine is on its way out but still showing a couple blips of heartbeat on the monitor," "dead" is "This wine has flatlined." Annoyingly, there's no surefire way to determine whether your wine is dead. Again, it helps if you've drunk that wine or wines from that producer or region several times before so at least you're familiar with what to expect. More likely than not it's old—not like "This bottle has been open for five days" old but "It was made twenty to thirty years ago" old—and without question, drinking it feels disappointing. Not enjoyable. Probably because you had high expectations of it, and they're not being met.

"I think this wine is dead, unfortunately. I've tried older vintages like this one before that showed beautifully, but this one just isn't giving anything."

Cheat Sheets

All right, dear friends, my burgeoning little wine nerds, this not-so-little vocabulary lesson has come to a close. That was fun! Hope you thought so, too, and if you're inspired to run out to the wine store or go meet your person at the wine bar to start putting all your newfound lingo to good use, I'll feel that I've done my job. Remember, don't expect that fluency in winespeak will come easily or all at once. It takes practice, and you can come back to this book time and again as you need it. Use it as your jumping-off point, find your own way with the words, have a good time with them, and trust your own palate and voice.

As a parting gift, in these last pages are some cheat sheets that I hope you'll find handy: things like a "do say this" and "don't say this" guide; a key to pronouncing tongue-twister grape names; food and wine pairing strategies; and suggestions for different tasting-notes terms that are frequently partnered together.

And with that I'll say cheers, here's to living life glass half full!

The Do Say This and Don't Say This Guide

Here's a list of things to say to help you sound in the know, plus some things *not* to say if you want to avoid sounding like a newb.

Do . . .

Ask to have your sparkling wine served in an AP (all-purpose) glass. Flutes and coupes are fun and festive, but if you want to really appreciate a sparkling wine's aromas and flavors, you need a glass that allows you to swirl the liquid and that you can stick your nose into.

Say "wine key" instead of "cork-screw." It'll make you sound as though you've been slinging bottles and pouring juice for years.

Be as descriptive as possible when asking for a wine recom-mendation. Please, *please*, don't just say you want a "nice," "smooth" wine. Give examples of wines you have (or haven't!) liked in the past. Give a price range. Talk about what you're going to be eating with the wine. Describe the vibe.

Ask about off-the-beaten-path grapes and regions whenever you see them. There are a couple of reasons for this. For one, it'll help you expand your knowledge—always a good thing. Two: It can be a great way to find deals. It's easy for places to get away with charging a little more for well-known grapes/producers/regions because, well, they're well-known. Supply and demand, baby. The "geekier" wines on a list or in a shop are probably there because the buyer loves them. But because they're not as popular, their prices tend to be kept at a friendlier price point to encourage curiosity and discovery.

Ask for certain reds to be served chilled and whites not to be served too chilled. Light-bodied, aromatic, low-tannin reds (think Gamay, Pinot Noir, Frappato, Cinsault, Trousseau, Valpolicella Classico) are fab when slightly chilled, around 55°F. It enhances their refreshingness and makes that fruit and acidity pop. P-o-p. That being said: Serve white wine—or any wine, for that matter—too cold, and you'll notice that . . . you're probably not noticing much. That's because at a certain point, the cold dulls the wine's aromas and flavors. It's recommended to serve lighter-bodied whites between 45° and 50°F and fuller-bodied whites in the 50°–55°F range.

Ask who imports the wines you like. Or at least get into the habit of turning the bottle around and checking out the back label, where it's listed. Finding out who imports the wines you consistently enjoy is kind of like finding a music or restaurant critic whose judgment you trust and whose taste aligns with your own. Having that as a tool in your back pocket can come in super handy when you're shopping for wine. Maybe you're looking for something from a particular region, but you don't recognize any of the producers. Or maybe you want to take a chance on trying something new and foreign to you. If it's imported by a company that brings in wines you've liked in the past, at least you can have reasonable confidence in the quality of the products it imports and know that your style preferences and philosophies vibe.

Don't . . .

Talk about a wine's "legs," aka "tears," aka those translucent droplets sliding down the side of the glass after you give your wine a swirl. They're the result of alcohol evaporating (please don't ask me to go into more detail; science was never my thing), and the quantity of droplets and speed at which they slide down can be used as indicators of the weight and alcohol content of the wine. The slower the drops move, the boozier and heavier the wine. But to be honest, it's a pretty old-timey term as far as usefulness and relevance go. As much as my dad (and dad jokesters) may have liked to compliment a wine for its "nice legs" (nudge, nudge, wink, wink), in fact it has no correlation with a wine's quality. Aside from maybe trying to assess a wine's legs to take a stab-in-the-dark guess at its alcohol content, like a kind of party trick, you can probably avoid using the term.

Say you only like pale rosés because darker rosés are sweeter. By all means, like a pale rosé if you like a pale rosé. But the deepness of the color is not an indication of the dryness level of the wine. It has more to do with the natural pigmentation of the grape skin and how much contact the juice (which is clear) has had with the grape skins.

Say that rosé is only a spring and summer wine. Keep pouring it all year round if you want to! It doesn't stop being delicious just because the temps outside have dropped. PS: It's a sleeper favorite food-pairing wine.

Say that red wine doesn't go with fish. This is an antiquated wine-food pairing rule of thumb. Sure, okay, you're probably not going to want to pour a big, jammy, oaky red when you're serving a delicate steamed filet of sole. But a Pinot Noir with roasted salmon or a Portuguese red with grilled octopus or seafood stew? Chef's kiss.

Say "This red is too sweet." Remember, unless it's a legit sweet or dessert wine, chances are that isn't technically true. Go with "fruit forward," "jammy," and/or "fruit bomb" instead.

Say "I hate Riesling because I only like dry whites." Womp, womp. Poor Riesling, it is so misunderstood. Despite however many sommeliers have been shouting it from the rooftops for years, the common perception (in the United States, at least), is that Riesling is a sweet wine. But most of the Riesling produced around the world is made in a *dry* style.

Ask for a "sulfite-free" wine.
All wines contain sulfites; they're a natural by-product of the wine-making process. It's better to say "I'm looking for a wine that doesn't have added sulfites." Basically, if this is really of concern, avoid buying wine in a grocery store or big-box wine shop and seek out wines that are made in a natural/low-intervention style.

Say "I hate all Chardonnay but love Chablis." Because pssssst . . . Chablis *is* Chardonnay (see page 239). The point here is: Don't be so quick to write off a grape variety. How it presents and drinks can vary dramatically based on where it's grown, the style of the region or producer, and other factors. It's like what people say about certain ingredients or foods: Maybe it's not that you don't like Brussels sprouts but that you just haven't yet found a way you like Brussels sprouts prepared.

Call a wine Champagne unless it actually comes from Champagne. "Sparkling wine" is the most accurate catchall term for any wine with fizz.

Say that a wine must be lower quality because it has a screw cap. You can find lots of great wine that isn't cork sealed, such as Grüner Veltliners from Austria and Sauvignon Blancs from New Zealand. Plus, you never have to worry about its being corked!

Try to help by moving your glass closer to the server right as they're about to pour your glass. Okay, this one's an action to avoid, not a statement, but it's a good one. They've lined up, they've taken aim, don't mess with the process by making the glass a moving target.

Grape Expectations: Getting to Know the Grapes Behind the Place-Names

It is all too easy to feel confused and overwhelmed when you're walking through a wine shop trying to pick out a bottle, especially if you're newer to the game. Something that makes it even more confusing: Some wines have the grape or grape blend listed on the label, but other ones don't. Some list just the region. Some list both. Maybe you're thinking *Okay, for real, am I being punked here? How am I supposed to know what it is?*

While New World wines make it nice and easy, typically listing the grape or grape blend somewhere on the label, Old World wines have more of a playing-hard-to-get thing going on. With European wines, the emphasis is much more on the winegrowing region and the prestige it carries, rather than the varietals. These regions, aka *appellations*, are government regulated, with specific winemaking guidelines in place, such as which varietal(s) can be used, to ensure the maintenance of quality standards and traditions.

While some Old World wines are moving toward listing varietals on the label in an effort to make themselves more approachable in the international market, it's worth familiarizing yourself with some of the more popular wines that are labeled by region. That way, when someone tries to tell you that they hate Sauvignon Blanc but love Sancerre, you can be like *snap snap* "Sancerre *is* Sauvignon Blanc."

Here are the names of appellations and the names of the dominant grape varietal(s) in wines from those regions.

Barbaresco: *Nebbiolo*

Barolo: *Nebbiolo*

Beaujolais: *Gamay*

Bordeaux (Right Bank—i.e., Pomerol, Saint-Émilion): *Merlot*

Bordeaux (Left Bank—i.e., Médoc, Saint-Julien, Margaux, Pauillac, Saint-Estèphe): *Cabernet Sauvignon*

Brunello di Montalcino: *Sangiovese*

Burgundy (red): *Pinot Noir*

Chablis (and almost all white wines made in Burgundy): *Chardonnay*

Châteauneuf-du-Pape: *Grenache, Syrah, Mourvèdre*

Chianti: *Sangiovese*

Chinon: *Cabernet Franc*

Condrieu: *Viognier*

Côtes du Rhône: *Grenache, Syrah, Mourvèdre*

Côte Rôtie: *Syrah*

Muscadet: *Melon de Bourgogne*

Priorat: *Grenache, Carignan*

Ribera del Duero: *Tempranillo*

Rioja (red): *Tempranillo*

Rioja (white): *Viura*

Sancerre (white): *Sauvignon Blanc*

Sancerre (rosé or red): *Pinot Noir*

Sauternes: *Sémillon*

Savennières: *Chenin Blanc*

Soave: *Garganega*

Tokaj: *Furmint*

Txakoli: *Hondarrabi Zuri*

Vouvray: *Chenin Blanc*

Xino-what?
How to Pronounce Grape Tongue Twisters

We've all been there: You're out to dinner, perusing the wine list, and when the server asks if you know what you'd like to order, you sweat and stammer awkwardly for a moment before going in for the trusty "hold up the menu and point" technique. Because that feels safer than potentially mispronouncing something and sounding like a totally unsophisticated wine newb.

With wine there will always be *How the eff do I say that word?* land mines: Where the wine is made, the producer, even the names of many grape varietals can be tongue twisters. Like, "Oh, yes, please, I'd like the Guh-whatchamacallit from Château Who Knows What in Couldn't Tell You Where, France." RIP your confidence.

So, to that end, here's a how-to-say-it guide to some of the trickiest-to-pronounce wine grape names.

White

Gewürztraminer: Guh-voortz-tra-mee-ner

Viognier: Vyoh-gnyay

Pedro Ximénez: Pay-droh Hee-meh-nez

Manzanilla: Man-zah-nee-yah

Assyrtiko: Ah-seer-tee-koh

Grüner Veltliner: Groo-ner Velt-lee-ner

Godello: Go-day-yoh

Verdejo: Vair-day-hoh

Moschofilero: Moh-skoh-fee-leh-roh

Melon de Bourgogne: Me-lohn duh Boor-goh-nyuh

Falanghina: Fah-lan-ghee-nah

Aligoté: Ah-lee-goh-tay

Rkatsiteli: Er-cat-tsee-teh-lee

Sémillon: Seh-mee-yawn

Red

Montepulciano: Mon-teh-pool-cha-noh

Tempranillo: Tem-prah-nee-yoh

Zweigelt: Tsvai-gelt

Blaufränkisch: Blaw-fren-kish

Mourvèdre: Moor-veh-druh

Cinsault: Sahn-soh

Carménère: Car-me-nair

Carignan: Cah-ree-nyawn

Xinomavro: Zee-no-mah-vroh

Agiorgitiko: Ay-yor-yee-tee-koh

Trousseau: Trou-soh

Pinot Meunier: Pee-no Muh-nyay

Aglianico: Ah-lee-yah-nee-koh

Is It Pinot Gris or Pinot Grigio?
Wine Grapes' Aliases

As you might have noticed, not all wine grapes operate under the same name when they travel internationally. For example, the grape that goes by Pinot Grigio in Italy is called Pinot Gris in France and the United States, Grauburgunder in German-speaking countries, and Sivi Pinot in Croatia and Slovenia.

Take a minute to familiarize yourself with these popular grapes' alternative names so that you never feel out of the loop. Note that when it's a grape's most commonly used international name, such as Pinot Noir or Syrah, not *aaaaall* of the countries that use that name are listed. For example, in the list here, Pinot Noir is used in France and the United States, but it is also called Pinot Noir in English-speaking countries such as Australia and New Zealand.

Mourvèdre (France): Monastrell (Spain), Mataro (Australia, occasionally California)

Grenache (France, US): Garnacha (Spain), Cannonau (Italy)

Chenin Blanc (France, US): Steen (South Africa)

Pinot Gris (France, US): Pinot Grigio (Italy), Grauburgunder (Germany, Austria), Sivi Pinot (Croatia, Slovenia)

Pinot Noir (France, US.): Pinot Nero (Italy), Spätburgunder (Germany, Austria)

Pinot Blanc (France, US): Pinot Bianco (Italy), Weissburgunder (Germany, Austria)

Muscat (France, US): Moscato (Italy), Zibibbo (Italy), Moscatel (Spain), Muskateller (Germany, Austria)

Trebbiano (Italy): Ugni Blanc (France)

Cabernet Franc (France, US): Bouchet, Breton (both also France)

Syrah (France, US): Shiraz (Australia)

Carignan (France): Cariñena (Spain), Mazuelo (Spain), Carignano (Italy)

Malbec (Argentina, US): Côt (France)

Zinfandel (US): Primitivo (Italy)

Nebbiolo (Italy): Spanna, Chiavennasca (both also Italy)

Albariño (Spain): Alvarinho (Portugal)

Preparing for Pairings: Food and Wine Pairing Strategies

All the "always drink this with that" and "never drink that with this" and questing for perfection has a tendency to make food and wine pairing feel daunting. In reality, it should be fun. The following are not rules (boo, rules), but some popular strategies and considerations to help guide you in what is hopefully a journey of playful and delicious experimentation.

Acid is your BFF.

If you remember only one thing about food and wine pairing, let it be this: In high-acid wines we trust. Acid refreshes your palate and provides contrast, so it helps balance food and makes flavors pop. It does it all.

Opposites attract.

The classic formula that's been working for rom-coms since the beginning of time also works for wine and food pairing. Some of the most popular unlikely love story combos include:

Acid with fatty or creamy foods: Think Champagne with fried chicken or Aligoté with seared scallops in a lemon butter sauce.

Bitter (high-tannin) with fatty foods: Nebbiolo with a porterhouse steak.

Sweet (or semisweet) with savory or salty or spicy foods: Think Sauternes with pâté de foie gras. (It's the most classic and overused pairing, I know. I don't care. It's bomb.) Or port with a super aged cheddar. Or an off-dry Riesling or Chenin Blanc with change-your-life-hot Szechuan or Thai dishes.

Likes can also attract.

This is the food and wine pairing equivalent of saying "I'm looking for someone who is my equal" on your dating profile. You can base a pairing on what the wine and a dish have in common. For example:

Do they share a dominant flavor characteristic you want to play up? For instance, a green veggie– or herb-centric dish with a wine that has green notes (Grüner Veltliner and Sauvignon Blanc, cough, cough).

Are they well matched in weight and/or flavor intensity? A softer, more delicate wine, for example, is likely to be overpowered by a heavy, boldly seasoned dish. And vice versa.

What about how the dish is cooked; is there an alignment between them? Drinking a richer, fuller-bodied wine is probably going to make more sense if you're roasting or braising, as opposed to steaming or lightly sautéing.

What grows together (often) goes together.

Your choice of wine may be inspired by the origin of your dish. Basically, it's the logic "If I were eating this dish in its homeland, what would I be drinking if I wanted to drink like a local?" It's not foolproof, and it really works only if the place the dish is from also produces wine. But still, it can be a fun, don't-overthink-it jumping-off point.

A few examples to get the inspo train rolling: a Tuscan-inspired wild boar pappardelle with Chianti; freshly shucked oysters on the half shell with Muscadet from France's Loire Valley; schnitzel with a dry Austrian or German Riesling;

Basque *pintxos* with citrusy-spritzy Txakoli; BBQ ribs with a California Zinfandel; black truffle risotto with earthy Piedmontese Nebbiolo . . . you get the idea.

Sometimes the secret is in the sauce.

Instead of focusing on the dish's main protein or veg, try using the sauce as your wine-pairing compass. It's kind of like the accessory that makes a dish's outfit, the reason you might choose to drink one thing with shrimp ceviche (a Vermentino or Albariño, perhaps?) and another with shrimp in a spicy green curry sauce (how about an off-dry Riesling or Chenin Blanc?).

Consider the occasion.

Try letting the vibe of the meal guide you. Are we talking casual, no-frills backyard barbecue, where all you need is a fun porch pounder (maybe a chilled Beaujolais-Villages) to match? Or will it be a fancy-schmancy treat yo'self celebration kind of affair, in which case you may want to bust out a baller bottle you've been saving? Or you can always just say "f*ck it" and go for the highbrow-lowbrow moment. A little Blanc de Blancs vintage Champagne with potato chips topped with crème fraîche and caviar? Sign. Me. Up.

Also consider the weather.

There's a reason we crave light, easy-drinking whites and rosés and chilled reds in the sweltering heat and hug-you-from-the-inside hearty reds and rich whites in cold weather.

Take inspo from the pros.

Take the opportunity to experience wine pairings at restaurants when you can. They're likely to introduce you to some cool and surprising combos and new wines, and you can hear the logic behind the choices from the sommelier.

When in doubt, pop some bubbs.

Sparkling wines have texture and plenty of acidity, and there is a wide range of styles and flavor profiles to choose from.

Avoid drinking . . .

Dry, high-acid wines with desserts. Not all opposites attract; the sweetness of the dish will make the wine taste scrunch-your-face sour.

High-tannin, high-ABV red wine with spicy foods. It will crank up the astringency and alcohol burn in the wine and make the spice in the dish go from "Okay, I can handle this" to The Last Dab hot.

High-tannin red wine with oily fish. Unless you enjoy a metallic aftertaste?

High-tannin red wine with bitter foods. Sometimes having one personality type in the relationship is enough. Bitter to the power of bitter does not equal balance; it equals too much bitter.

Partner up! Tasting-Notes Terms That Pair Well Together

Like peanut butter and jelly or macaroni and cheese, some words were made to go together. Here are some examples of tasting-notes terms that are frequently paired. Use them as inspiration to get the juices flowing as you get started on your wine-speaking journey.

Opens with, greets you with, offers up, hits you in the face with, bursting with +
- on the [x, y, z]
- bouquet or perfume of

Out of the gate or off the bat +
- one of the personality types
- bursting with or hits you with or offers up or greets you with

Notes of + on the [x, y, z]

Nose + quiet or loud (or explosive, bursting with).

On the palate + firm or stiff or grippy

Complex or cerebral +
- balanced
- layered
- haunting

Quiet or muted + over the hill

Needs air/time to open up/to unfurl/breathe +
- quiet
- shy
- tight
- closed
- reduced

Needs time in bottle + closed or muted

Tight or closed + totally different animal

Jammy or fruit bomb +
- fat
- flabby
- heavy
- rich
- big
- flamboyant
- hedonistic or opulent
- generous

Fruit forward +
- generous
- jammy
- juicy

Earthy +
- mineral driven
- savory
- forest floor
- funky

Funky +
- earthy
- barnyardy
- rustic

Oaky + buttery + creamy

Toasty + brioche

Lean +
- bright
- acid driven
- chiseled
- crunchy
- crisp
- restrained

Juicy +
- bright
- fleshy

Round +
- rich
- smooth
- creamy
- generous

Inky +
- rich
- concentrated

Awkward +
- angular
- messy

Flat +
- thin
- hollow

Rich +
- creamy
- velvety
- opulent
- hedonistic

Smooth or dances across the palate +
- silky
- fine grained
- elegant

Big +
- chewy
- rich

In a great spot or singing or open for business + balanced

Friendly and approachable or peppy +
- bright
- lively
- crushable or porch pounder

Elegant +
- restrained
- polished

Corked +
- muted
- dead
- flat

Flat + hollow

Any words for f*ck-ton of acidity (racy, zippy, electric, punchy, ripping) +
- chiseled
- lean

Reduced + blow off

Short + one note

What'd You Call Me?
A Grape Word Association Guide

The fact that wine judgments and assessments have basically no absolutes makes this a really tricky list to compile. Some Chardonnays are going to be lean and mineral driven; others oaky, rich, and buttery. You can find Syrahs that are all savory bacon fat and black pepper, just as you can find others that are fruit forward and jammy. It's important to approach wine tasting with an open mind, ready for discovery. But to help get the ball rolling, here are some tasting notes that are more or less commonly associated with some of the world's major wine grapes.

Chardonnay: Dry; oaky, buttery, rich, round, creamy, toasty, opulent (for a "classic" California kind of expression); lean, chiseled, f*ck-ton of acidity, savory, mineral driven (for a Burgundy style)

Sauvignon Blanc: Dry; pyrazine; crisp; lean; any of the f*ck-ton of acidity words; mineral driven

Pinot Gris: Crisp and lean or juicy and fleshy (depending on the style); friendly and approachable

Grüner Veltliner: Dry; crisp; lean; any of the f*ck-ton of acidity words; pyrazine

Albariño: Dry; lean; mineral driven (specifically, salty/saline); chiseled; lively; any of the f*ck-ton of acidity words; bright

Chenin Blanc: Dry, off dry, or sweet and lean or rich (depending on the style); any of the f*ck-ton of acidity words; lanolin; oily; bright; concentrated

Riesling: Dry, off dry, or sweet (depending on the style); any of the f*ck-ton of acidity words; mineral driven (specifically slate and petrol); juicy

Gewürztraminer: Loud; jumping out of the glass; huge nose; explosive; perfume; fleshy; juicy; concentrated

Pinot Noir: Bright; fine grained; savory; forest floor; elegant; mineral driven; lively; elegant

Nebbiolo: Grippy; firm; chewy; earthy; savory; bright; needs time to (breathe, unfurl); mineral driven; leathery; loud

Sangiovese: Rustic; savory; earthy; bright; lively; firm

Cabernet Franc: Pyrazine; earthy; savory; firm; mineral driven (often charred smoky); bright

Syrah: Savory (specifically meaty and black peppery) and earthy or fruit forward and jammy (depending on the style); firm; chewy

Tempranillo: Oaky (specifically American oak, dill, and coconut aromas); firm; savory; leathery; lively

Zinfandel: Fruit forward; jammy; inky; rich; concentrated; big; flexing; generous

Malbec: Fruit forward (although some can be made in an earthy style); jammy; smooth; concentrated; velvety; rich; generous

Cabernet Sauvignon: Fruit forward (more New World style) or earthy and savory (more Old World style); big; rich; velvety; oaky; inky; firm; chewy; muscular; hedonistic or flamboyant; opulent

Acknowledgments

This book is the realization of a nearly decade-long dream that I had honestly given up hope would ever come to fruition.

First and foremost, thank you to all the people who have enjoyed and supported @Freshcutgardenhose throughout the years. It's because of you that this became so much more than what it started out as: just some silly "drunk doodles" for the 'gram, a fun little hobby for a young wine nerd. Among these supporters, I would like to give the most special of shout-outs to Bill Jensen of Reveler's Hour in Washington, DC. Thank you, thank you, *thank you* for wallpapering your restaurant's bathrooms with my illustrations. I've connected with so many wonderful and unexpected people because of it, including my agent, Andrianna deLone.

Thank you, Andrianna, for sharing my vision and helping set this whole thing in motion.

I am also infinitely grateful to the incredibly talented team at Simon Element, especially my fantastic editors, Samantha Weiner and Emily Graff. Your enthusiasm, encouragement, and guidance have been invaluable. You helped me take this crazy concept and bring it to life in a way that's better than I could ever have imagined.

To my mom, my family, and my friends, words cannot begin to express how lucky I feel to have you in my corner, cheering me on with your unwavering love. Thank you for every "You got this" and "Don't worry, it's going to be great!" that you knew I needed to hear. And, in particular, thank you to Annie, Laura, Jess, and Julia for reading early drafts and being trusted sounding boards.

And last but not least, to my hunny, my Mousse, my best friend and husband, Jon: I literally could not have done this without you. You held this pregnant, hormonal, wine-deprived version of me together through the entirety of this project. Thank you for pushing me to keep writing and drawing when I really, *really* didn't want to. For weathering every meltdown. For believing in me even more than I believe in myself. You motivate and inspire me. I love you.

Index

About the Author

Maryse Chevriere is a writer, wine professional, and illustrator living in Boston, Massachusetts. A certified sommelier, Maryse's career in wine has spanned across New York City, San Francisco, and Boston, where she has enjoyed roles as a retail consultant, restaurant wine director, and distribution sales representative. Her witty, whimsical "drunk doodles" have been published in print and online in *Bon Appétit, Food & Wine, Wine Enthusiast,* and more. Her printed work has appeared in restaurants and wine bars in New York City; Washington, DC; Boston; and London. In 2016, her Instagram account @Freshcutgardenhose was honored with a prestigious James Beard Award in the category of humor and, in 2020, was nominated as a finalist for an IACP Digital Media Award. Maryse is a fervent proponent of living life glass (at least) half full, and believes that learning and talking about wine should be as accessible and fun as drinking it is.